SAVED HOT MESS

A Devotional for the Imperfect

By Mahogani Reign

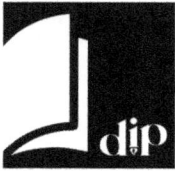

Saved Hot Mess: A Devotional for the Imperfect
By Mahogani Reign

ISBN: 978-0-9894423-5-0

Edited by: Christian Cashelle
Photography: Suzy Gorman

Manufactured in the United States of America

I dedicate this body of work to the ultimate matriarch, the one who has loved me whether saved or messy...my nurturing mother, Kayelle. You showed me the endless love of God through your grace for me.

I'd also like to acknowledge my beautiful children and Everlasting Village, from giving me the space to write in peace to listening to me dream in "the middle of a panoramic". You ALL will make it to heaven for loving me.

TABLE OF CONTENTS

PREFACE

I think it's safe to say that all of us now know how it feels to go through something. The pandemic has been a great hit to us all spiritually, physically, and emotionally. Our land is hurting. I have felt so helpless since the start of the pandemic and often wondered in what way could I help.

Personally, I have been navigating some of the most trying times of my life and all I wanted was for someone to come and help me. Even though I have a great support system, I felt like I still wasn't finding resolution or a resource to help me weather my complicated life. There wasn't a church to run to or a manual on how to maneuver my mess with my specific circumstances in mind. I felt so distraught.

Like the empath I am, I understand that others may be going through what I was going through. I needed to write this book so no one else will feel how I felt without a resource.

Imperfect people, like me, who love the Lord but cuss a little still have a purpose. When I turned to traditional devotionals, as beautiful as they were, they didn't really resonate with me. I haven't quite perfected the art of quoting bible verses and I'm surely no theologist. I was over here struggling with sin. I enjoyed having a few drinks. I didn't see the real harm with the occasional hookup. And forgiveness in my eyes was just about cutting people off. What was the harm in that? What did the Bible say about those things? What did God think about me not loving my body? These were all questions burning in my soul. I felt guilty about these thoughts mostly because they all seemed taboo or ungodly. I know for a fact that God wouldn't put me in a world full of sin and not give me the tools to navigate it. So, I went on a spiritual journey and searched the Word for answers to my burning questions and scantily clad issues.

I realized that not only could God use my saved, messy self but most of the people He used in the Bible were saved hot messes as well. Even the most beloved had a past that included murder, prostitution, betrayal, stealing, lying, cheating, and unbelief. If God could use these messy folks, surely He can use me...surely He can use us.

So, I challenge you to have a sense of purpose as you read this book for the next 28 days. Use this as an opportunity to have one on one time with God. Gather a group of friends and collectively bring your mess to God. I know I've gotten my biggest blessings and brightest ideas right after a successful fast and devotional journey. Always remember, no matter how far you stray, you are always His favorite child. (word to L.H.) He will leave the 99 for the 1. I'm claiming in advance a life changing breakthrough for you and me both. Time to get messy.

1

ADDICTED TO HURT - SAVED HOT MESS -

Face it, friend, we are all here for the same reason. One commonality we share is that we are no strangers to pain. Pain and hurt are naturally-occurring emotions and feelings that are necessary to shape our personalities and customize our human experience. When something hurts us, we *should* learn what to avoid, you know? It's admirable to turn your L into a lesson.

What about those of us who pick the L right back up, fully well knowing it only wants to destroy us? For example, I love spicy food. I don't care if it's a flavorful, zesty burrito or an overkill of sriracha hot sauce on some crispy wings. All I know is that I crave it and I love the way it excites my senses, clears my nose, and tingles the roof of my mouth. However, when I was pregnant with my youngest I was diagnosed with acid reflux. All the spicy food I ate started to take a toll as soon as it hit my stomach and caused me to choke in my sleep. As afraid as I was when I was awakened by acid flooding my airways and gasping for air mid-sleep, I'd find myself (sometimes as early as the next day) face to face with something else spicy.

I've also been spiritually hard headed with relationships and important decisions. There are things and people that God has placed "off limits" for me. They serve no purpose in my elevation or plan and in fact go against my calling. Somehow, even after I feel the divine ban, I still want the temporary satisfaction. I remember dating a man who was so toxic for me. He lied, cheated, stole, manipulated, was extremely jealous of me, and made countless broken promises. The more he let me down, the more I tried to be better for him. I had gotten so used to being mistreated that I longed for it. If he and I had a good day, I would brace myself for the pain I was used to receiving. Can you imagine the torture of pain being more normal than peace? For every moment of light and encouragement there was a darkness and negativity that loomed. In my right mind I knew I didn't want the hurt, but I knew it so well that I unknowingly willed it into my life. I dare say I invited it in.

Anticipating hurt for so long made me question if I was addicted to it. I realized I had a terrible tendency to self-sabotage. I would either invite hurtful things or feelings into my life or beat myself up so badly and wallow in self-blame. Whether it's a relationship with food, men, or anything else, we should never continue on a path of self-sabotage. At some point we must learn to see ourselves the way God sees us. He sees us as a vessel that He can use for His glory. If we put our faith in Him and put effort into fulfilling His will, it will break the cycle of being addicted to pain and hurt. God rewards us with refuge and peace in our relationship with Him. He provides a loving relationship that affirms and grows our spirit. Instead of negative cycles, God reaches us through positive reinforcement and divine chastising. So step out of that cycle, friend. The water feels so much better over here.

PSALM 34:11-22 NRSV

"Come, O children, listen to me; I will teach you the fear of the Lord. Which of you desires life, and covets many days to enjoy good? Keep your tongue from evil, and your lips from speaking deceit. Depart from evil, and do good; seek peace, and pursue it. The eyes of the Lord are on the righteous, and his ears are open to their cry. The face of the Lord is against evildoers, to cut off the remembrance of them from the earth. When the righteous cry for help, the Lord hears, and rescues them from all their troubles. The Lord is near to the brokenhearted, and saves the crushed in spirit. Many are the afflictions of the righteous, but the Lord rescues them from them all. He keeps all their bones; not one of them will be broken. Evil brings death to the wicked, and those who hate the righteous will be condemned. The Lord redeems the life of his servants; none of those who take refuge in him will be condemned."

PRAYER

Father God,

Amidst all of my inconsistencies and brokenness, You remain the same. Thank You for being a constant in my life. Thank You for not giving up on me and seeing me in a brighter light than I see myself. Please forgive me for my sins and shortcomings. Now that my hands are clean, please reset my spiritual taste buds. I've become entangled in a cycle of pain and hurt. I refuse to remain in this cycle anymore, Lord. I believe in You to retrain my heart. Retrain my desires and help me to turn away from things and people that no longer serve me. I present myself a living sacrifice to Your will and would rather have Your endless love. Come against anything or anyone who disrupts me from fulfilling Your prophecy over my life. I claim healing over being addicted to hurt and I praise You in advance for the victory.

In the mighty and matchless name of Jesus, amen.

CLEANSING THOUGHT

It's healing season. Period. I made up my mind that I will live a life of prosperity, joy, and hope. I can't control the things that happened to me, that shaped me, and made me fall prey to habits of self-sabotaging. However, I can be proactive and prevent it from reigning in my future. I'm not doing it alone. You are coming with me. It's so important that we go through "Hurt Rehab" together. Misery loves company but healing is infectious. God loves us in all of our imperfections and quirks. By His stripes, we are healed.

---

1. Do you find yourself in repetitive, hurtful situations? Identify them.
2. Have you consulted with God about how to navigate repetitive, hurtful cycles?

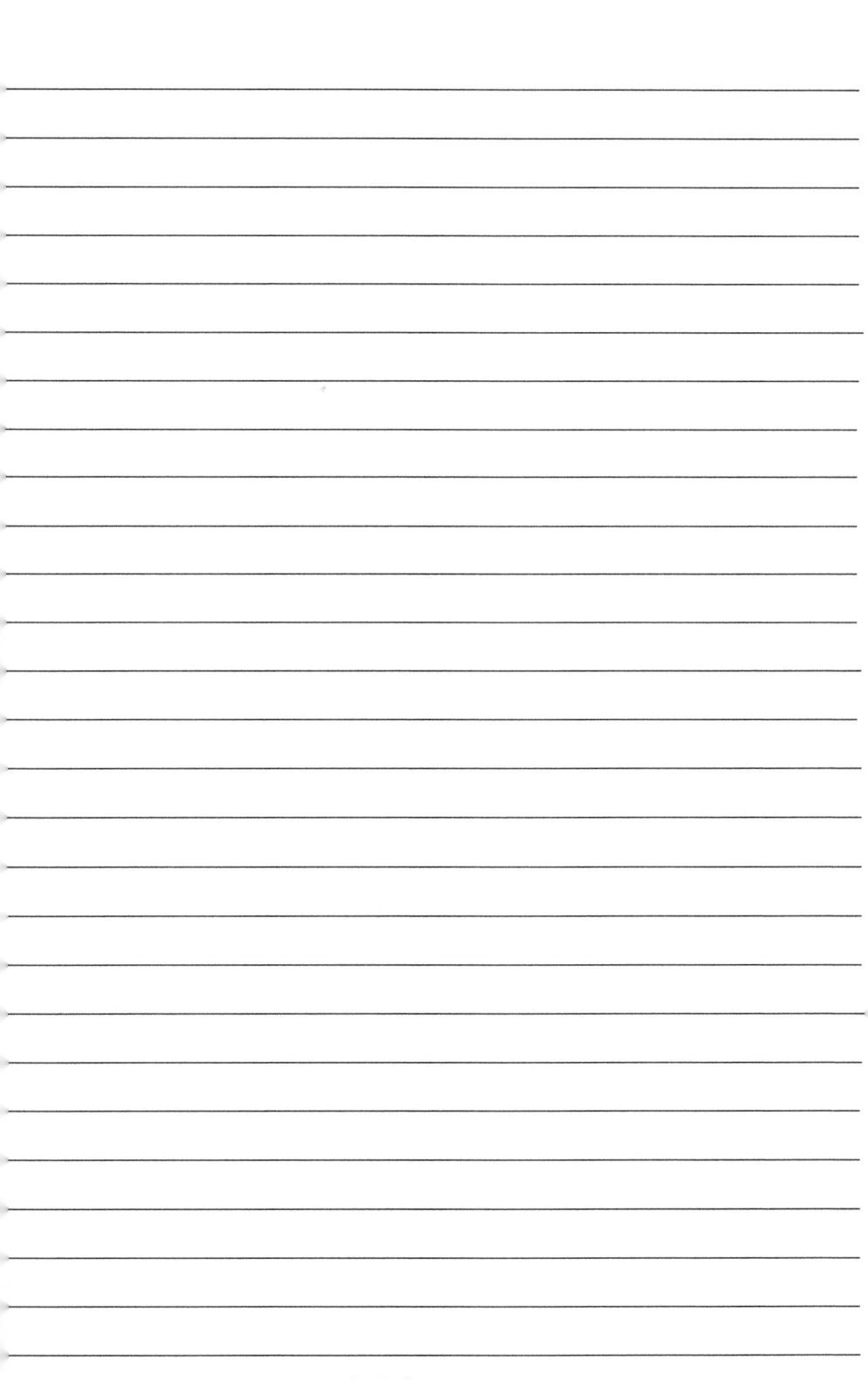

2

UNFAILING LOVE-SAVED HOT MESS-HIS-

When Oscar Hammerstein II wrote the lyrics to "My Favorite Things" I wonder if he had a clue how much of a sentimental staple his song would become. Every Christmas, we are sure to hear the classic tune paint a picture of seeing the bright side of things; envisioning our glasses half full. I enjoy hearing the cutesy Hallmark imagery with minor chords leading the way. The final verse is by far my favorite. He wrote, "When the dog bites, when the bee stings, when I'm feeling sad I simply remember my favorite things and then I don't feel so bad." (If you held that "sooooo" in your head I just wanted to give you a fist bump for the culture.)

After reading up on the lyricist, I found out that he died one year after he wrote the song. Hammerstein never got to experience what we feel when we hear that song echo throughout department stores during the holiday season. Remembering this tune made me think of some of my favorite things that have the power to make my problems feel smaller. I think of the smell of the heat getting turned on for the first time of the year after the weather changes from warm to cold. I think of the satisfaction and warmth I get when my children smile together. I think of MAC Cosmetics' Mineralize Skin finish Natural baked powder and how brushing it all over my face makes my makeup feel like a masterpiece. As much as I love all of these things, nothing compares to the love I have for the Master of Change.

Nothing compares to the great I Am. God's love is unfailingly, permanent, and perfect. Countless times I have cried out to God after feeling like the love I had for others wasn't reciprocated. I understood that the love people would have for me had flaws and conditions. However, I also had to learn that my need to receive a return on the love I had for others was flawed as well. God created love to be a balancer; a solution for everything. He didn't create it to be a gambling tool to use to get our way. Agape love or divine love is the type of love God has for us and He expects us to love each other the same way. As we strive to love better, we must acknowledge God's unfailing love for us. He loves us through mistakes, disappointments, and when we don't deserve it. He does not withhold it out of spite. God's love is my most favorite thing. His love makes everything not feel soooooooo bad.

1 CORINTHIANS 13:8-13 NRSV

"Love never ends. But as for prophecies, they will come to an end; as for tongues, they will cease; as for knowledge, it will come to an end. For we know only in part, and we prophesy only in part; but when the complete comes, the partial will come to an end. When I was a child, I spoke like a child, I thought like a child, I reasoned like a child; when I became an adult, I put an end to childish ways. For now we see in a mirror, dimly, but then we will see face to face. Now I know only in part; then I will know fully, even as I have been fully known. And now faith, hope, and love abide, these three; and the greatest of these is love."

PRAYER

Father God, thank You for love. Thank You for creating and cultivating love. If I have ever misused love or misappropriated love, please forgive me. I repent of my sins. I invite You into my life to have Your way. Make anew what I have tainted as well as what has tainted me. Help me to love those close to me as well as those I have discordances with. Allow me to be a living testimony of what it looks like to be loved by You. Help me to trust Your love more so that Your will for me can be done. I love You with all of my mind, heart, and being. In Jesus' name, amen.

CLEANSING THOUGHT

God's love is perfect. We must always aim to love like Him. His word maps out what pure love should look and feel like. So when we love we should do it with patience, kindness, without envy, without boasting or harboring pride. The embodiment and daily practice of pure love is a sure way to connect us to God. As you go through the motions, make sure you include love in everything that you do. God has and is certainly doing it for us.
Btw, I love you.

1.   Describe how God shows His love for you. Get personal.
2.   How do you show God your appreciation for His unfailing love?

T rust is so precious, so pivotal, and so important. It's a foundational emotion and a necessary building block for any and every relationship. Even a newborn baby understands the concept of trust. The baby learns fairly quickly that their cries and discontent will give them whatever they want and they trust that they will receive it. I have seen trust create and foster some of the most beautiful unions ever. I've also seen broken trust tear down families and legacies without a second thought.

Trust usually looks like one person having an expectation for another person to be reliable, worthy, and honest. In turn, that person follows through on the expectations set for them. Honesty is foundational when it comes to trust. Just recently I had to come to a difficult realization that I, a person that publicly proclaims to hate lies, likes to be lied to. I mean, I don't stand up on the mountain tops and scream, "Hey you, come lie to me!" I do, however, allow people that have shown themselves as liars continue to have the opportunity to further deceive me. I give every excuse in the world so I can continue to be manipulated. It's sad really. The pain of confronting people that I learned to revere, respect, and love is so hard. The character associated with a liar is so detrimental and low-vibrating, it feels disloyal to associate a loved one with it. I prefer to think highly of the people that I love, even if I know they haven't been honest with me. I also believe they have the opportunity to be better. I call myself extending grace. Listen Beloved, God wants us to have grace but He does not want us to be a fool for anyone. Chances are, if God let it be known that the person is deceiving us, we are expected to stand up for obedience and righteousness. We have to call them out. God wants much more for us than to be bound to imposters living false realities and selling fake news.

EPHESIANS 5:6-14

"Let no one deceive you with empty words, for because of these things the wrath of God comes on those who are disobedient. Therefore do not be associated with them. For once you were darkness, but now in the Lord you are light. Live as children of light— for the fruit of the light is found in all that is good and right and true. Try to find out what is pleasing to the Lord. Take no part in the unfruitful works of darkness, but instead expose them. For it is shameful even to mention what such people do secretly; but everything exposed by the light becomes visible, for everything that becomes visible is light. Therefore it says, "Sleeper, awake! Rise from the dead, and Christ will shine on you.""

PRAYER

Dear God of truth and light, thank You for Your goodness to me. Thank You for giving me a spiritual mirror. Thank You for Your correction. Lord, release me from the guilt and shame I feel for trusting someone who is unworthy. Restore my confidence and help me listen to that small, still voice that tells me when something isn't right. I know I'm not perfect but You are; I want to be more like You. Thank You for forgiving me of my transgressions, especially the ones I invited into my life. Lord, I ask that You strengthen me to live in my truth no matter how uncomfortable it might be. Please rebuke lies and false information that may have intentions of derailing Your plans for me. Help me to see clearer and sharpen my discernment in the days ahead. In Jesus' name, amen.

CLEANSING THOUGHT

Unfortunately, many of us can relate to the title of this chapter. Our self-esteem has been measured by our abilities. The truth is, if we measured our esteem on how perfect God is and how He sees us, we could trust ourselves and our decisions. If we truly acknowledge God for His majesty we wouldn't be so desperate to accept the lies and deception of others. It's time to vibrate where God intended us to be all along.

1.   Would you prefer a gentle white lie, or a harsh, dark truth? Explain why.
2.   Have you ever prayed to God about telling the truth and/ or asked forgiveness for telling a lie?

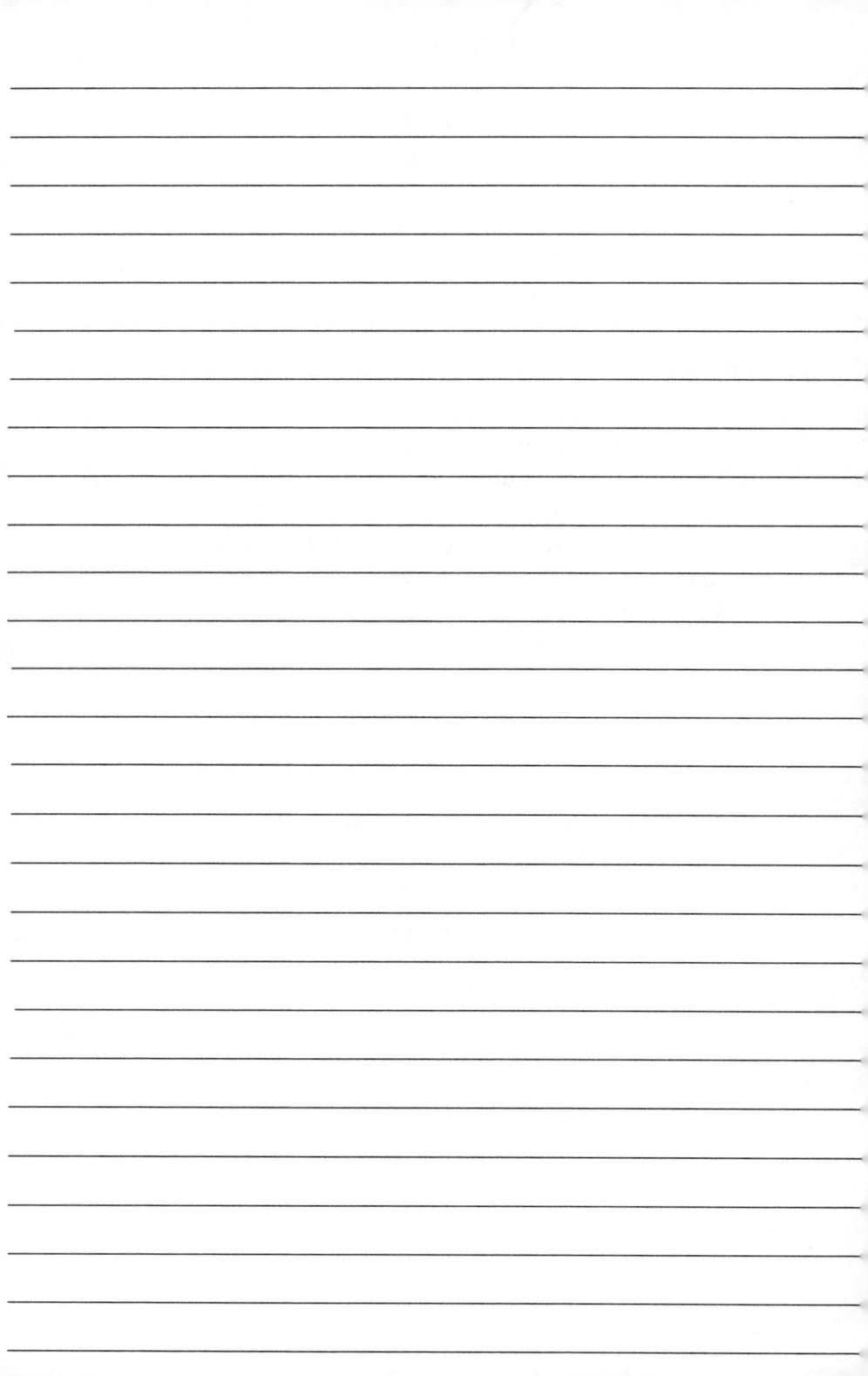

RED LIGHTS-SAVED HOT MESS-DIVINE

4

E veryone can relate to the headache of rush hour traffic. Nothing is worse than every car in the city on the road at the same time, yearning for a "line leader" position but stuck between the same cars for what feels like forever. Every driver assumes that their desire to arrive at their destination is more important than the next driver's. In the meantime, the seatbelt starts to get uncomfortable along with everything else in our bodies because patience is so 2018. The time starts dwindling away minute by minute. We were just 10 minutes away from our destination but now the ETA is 15. Then the holy grail of irritants shows its face...the short lived green arrow appears for all of 15 seconds with just enough time for 3 cars to turn and then boom! Red light! It's bad enough to be slowed down but to be brought to a halt just when I thought I was getting somewhere is so frustrating.

It reminds me of the way God throws a wrench in my plans when I believe they are fail-proof. There was a time when the bank froze my account due to a privacy breach. I begged them to lift the hold so I could blow my money how I pleased, but my begging and pleading didn't work against God's divine judgement for my life. What I couldn't see was the emergency ahead of me. I would need that money a few days later. All three of my children were diagnosed with strep throat and needed medication. That hit my household like an unexpected tsunami. I had to take off work, wash all of the bedding, buy soup, make emergency doctor visits, and purchase medicine. God allowing the bank to temporarily freeze my money was Him being a divine red light.

I can endlessly recount the times that I wanted to do something, whether it was foolish or even logical in my eyes, but God had a better plan, a fool-proof plan, an all-knowing plan. God is omnipresent. He sees our past, present, and future all at the same time. It's difficult for us to understand because unlike Him, we can only see our past and a portion of our present. Yielding to God's all-knowing power is the key to having our future secured.

ISAIAH 43:15-19

"I am the Lord, your Holy One, the Creator of Israel, your King. Thus says the Lord, who makes a way in the sea, a path in the mighty waters, who brings out chariot and horse, army and warrior; they lie down, they cannot rise, they are extinguished, quenched like a wick: Do not remember the former things, or consider the things of old. I am about to do a new thing; now it springs forth, do you not perceive it? I will make a way in the wilderness and rivers in the desert."

PRAYER

Holy, eternal, and omnipresent God, thank You. Thank You for protecting me from the unseen dangers and obstacles that have tried to derail me. Please forgive me for not trusting You in the past. I am only human and cannot fathom all of the glory and wisdom You hold. Please eliminate the spirit of fear and selfish ambition that has come between us. I invite You to have full reign over my life and my decisions. I ask You to remove anything out of my life that is not in line with Your plans for me. Give me the strength to adjust my focus to You and my destiny in Your will. In Jesus' name, amen.

CLEANSING THOUGHT

God be knowing (yes, I said be knowing) what He's doing. Nothing is wrong with being a hustler and wanting more out of life. But worldly ambition can be a roadblock or distraction to our destiny. If we quiet our personal desires, open our hearts and seek God's advice, our pathway will be more clear. We all get a sign before we go against God's will but it's up to us to listen. When God ceases something, no matter how much we want it, we must obey. Because He will do what He said He would, whether we are on board or not.

---

1. Name a specific time when you felt God stopped you from doing something.
2. What have been some consequences for going against God's orders to stop? Give Examples.

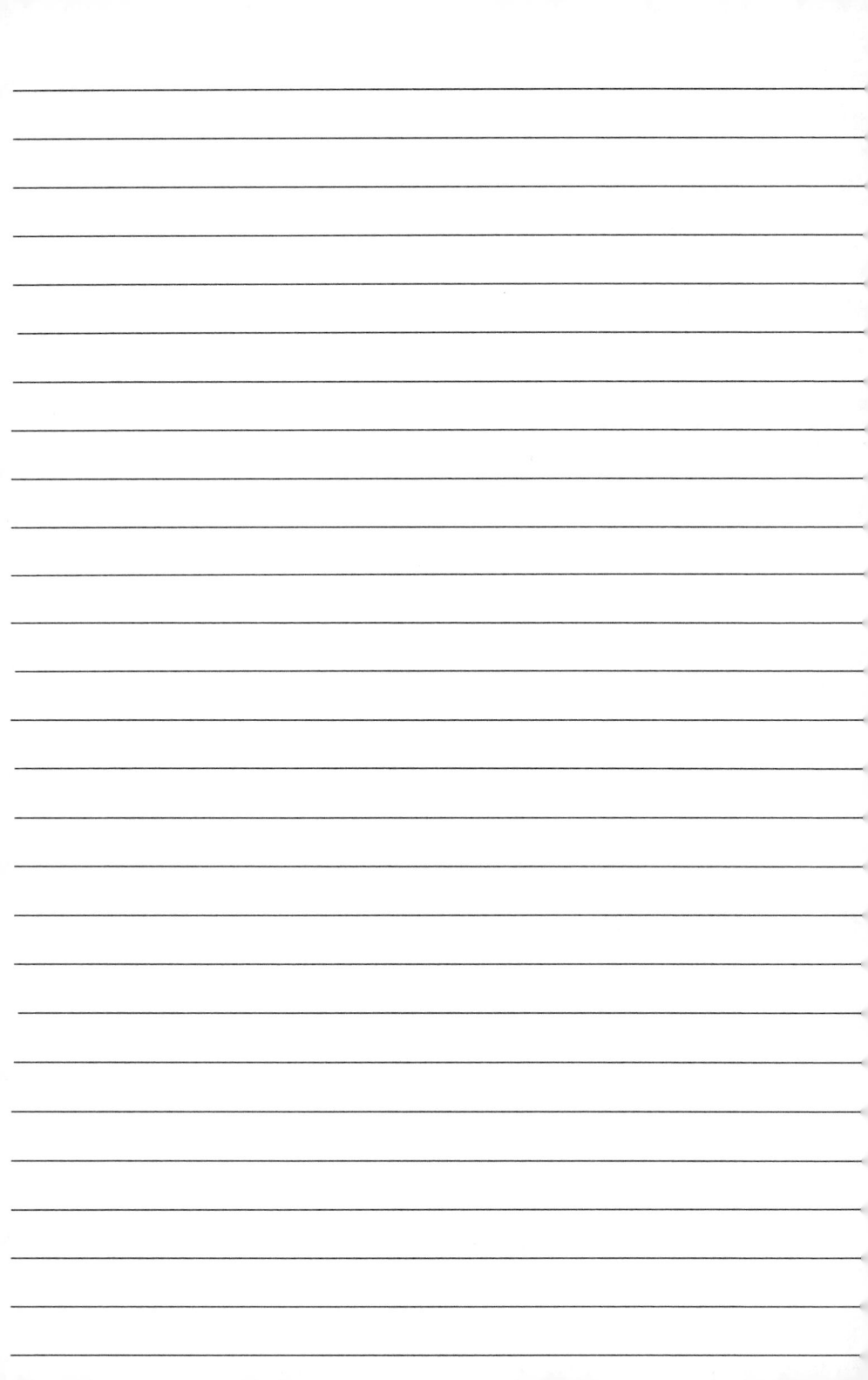

FRIENDS-SAVED HOT MESS - SELF-WORTHY

5

We are getting to the part of the devotional where you're probably saying, "friend, you don't know my life!" That means it's working! A cut stings once you put alcohol on it, but it's part of the healing process right? So, on to the topic of friendship. When the great Aubrey Graham, also known as Drake, released "No New Friends" and "Fake Love" I realized the art of friendship was being tainted. "Friend" was once an earned title associated with trustworthiness, loyalty, and commitment. The Bible even urges us to understand the friend we have in Jesus. Then social media showed up and lowered the value of friendship to lurking on controlled content and filtering every freaking thing to death.

Healthy boundaries are a thing of the past and "friends" now care more about the appearance of the friendship than they care about the quality of the friendship. I'll never wag my finger without putting myself in the hot seat. So I'll admit that I've done it, too. I've taken offense to people not liking my photos. I've Facetuned my imperfections and amplified my better qualities. I've paid attention to which of my friends could master the art of "make it look good" trickery and looked at them as more of an asset than my friends that were not as social media savvy.

I've been a selfie-worthy friend. There have been many times that I've outwardly looked like I had it going on. Hair and edges laid, makeup beat, outfit snatched, yet broken to pieces on the inside. I had nothing to offer my friendships during those moments except a selfie. God put us on the earth together to be more than just snapshots of unfulfilling moments. He gave us all of the similarities we have so that we can connect to one another. God gave us recollection of our mistakes so that we can share our testimonies with one another and learn from each other's trials. Putting on the facade of a perfect life does no justice to the kingdom of God. Iron sharpens iron, not iron-plated plastic.

It has taken all 30 years of my life for me to appreciate my noble friends. They are usually MIA for gossip and partying, but are front and center when I'm experiencing heartache or loss. My selfie-worthy friends are the exact opposite. They are temporary leeches that were never meant to be real friends. It's our fault when we upgrade a leech to a friend. When we get hurt or they run us dry, we act surprised. All that leech did was be itself. Save yourself some heartache, resources, and time by being selective and honest about who you invite to be a part of your journey. Be the energy you want your friends to reciprocate. Don't let your poor judgement be the reason you give up on meaningful friendships. There are friendships in the balance, right now, waiting to blossom. Sometimes we have to come out of our comfort zone. Society has placed markers like race, age, socioeconomic ability, and class between us. I challenge everyone, including me, to open our horizons. Let's be intentional about cultivating healthy, like-minded relationships that may not align with what we are used to but line up wholly with our purpose and who we really are.

JOHN 15:12-17

"This is my commandment, that you love one another as I have loved you. No one has greater love than this, to lay down one's life for one's friends. You are my friends if you do what I command you. I do not call you servants any longer, because the servant does not know what the master is doing; but I have called you friends, because I have made known to you everything that I have heard from my Father. You did not choose me but I chose you. And I appointed you to go and bear fruit, fruit that will last, so that the Father will give you whatever you ask him in my name. I am giving you these commands so that you may love one another."

PRAYER

Father God, thank You for being a true friend to me. After all of my shortcomings and transgressions, You are still faithful. Please forgive me for not allowing You to pick my friends. My fleshly desires are strong but You are stronger. I pray for keener discernment regarding those I invite into my life. Help me to attract who I need in order to better live within Your will. In Jesus' name, amen.

CLEANSING THOUGHT

The qualifications for friendship should never start with how someone looks in a picture with you. Clout is cheap. In order to have true friends you must be one. A true friend is a priceless asset that some may never get a chance to experience. If you have at least one good friend, outside of Jesus of course, cherish them with all of your heart. Be aware of those that come into your life with ill intentions. If you play your cards right they will just pass you by. Everyone isn't invited to where God wants you to go.

1.   What is your personal definition of friendship?
2.   Based on your personal definition, are *you* a good friend?

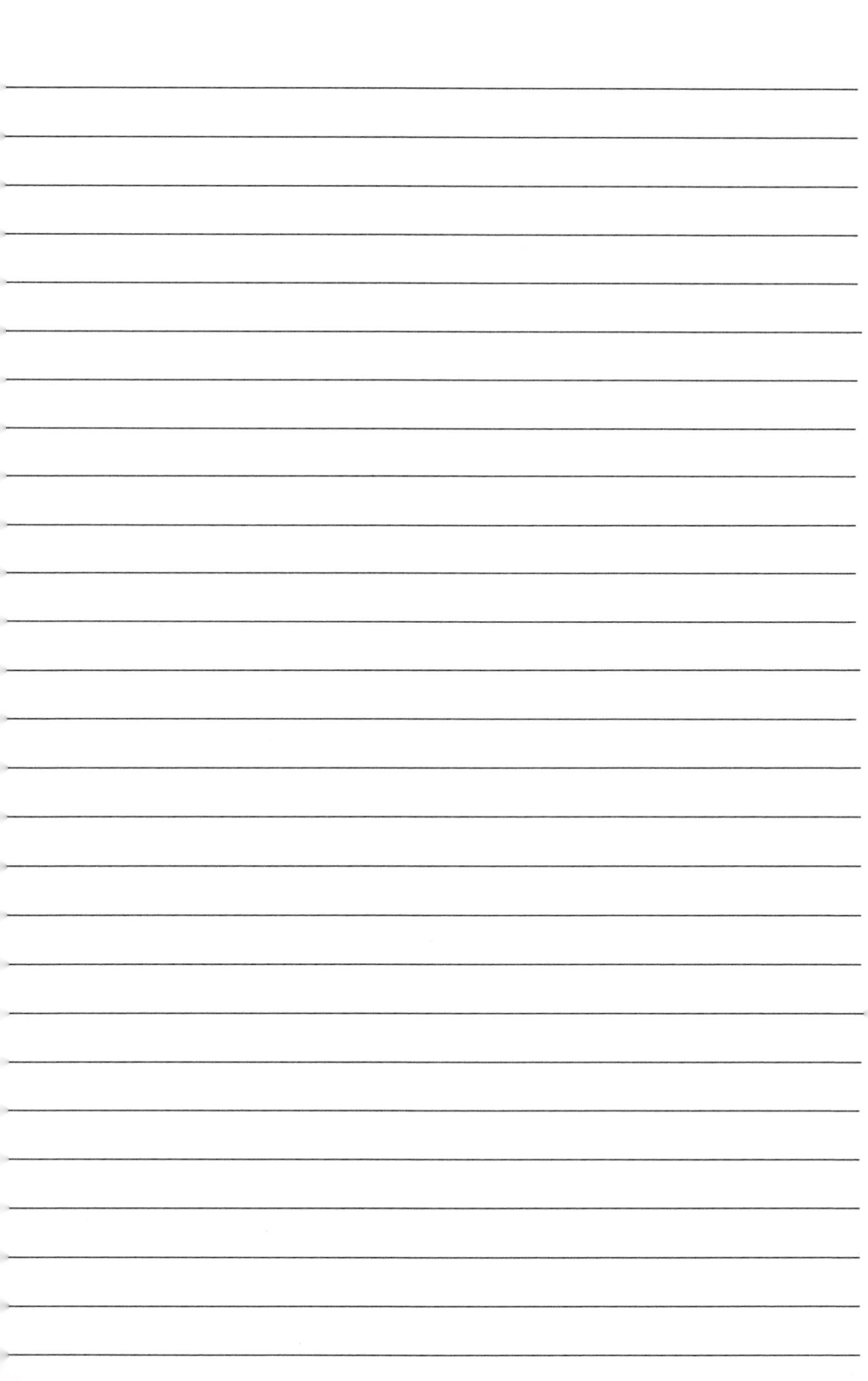

6

Worship is usually viewed as a grandiose gesture reserved for larger than life deities. The only one that I consciously worship is Jehovah God. I worship God by lifting my hands, singing praises, and at times I even allow my tears to speak for me. Until I took a deeper look at my actions and intent, I thought I was a devout worshipper that would never break the first commandment of God. Unconsciously, throughout my life I made the mistake of worshipping smaller, idle, quasi-gods.

The first mistake I noticed was I made my mother a quasi-god. I was so obsessed with making my mother proud of me. It was no fault of hers; there was a rush I got just knowing that she was proud. In the event that I did disappoint her it would derail my entire day and sometimes my whole week. Soon enough that obsession trickled into my friendships and relationships. I would wake up in the morning and the first thing on my mind would be how to make the day better for all my little quasi-gods. I kept an unofficial list of making sure they all got their due praises. If agreeing with them meant going against my own good judgement or preference, oh well. Eventually, I turned social media and my business into gods as well. I would barely wake up before I was scrolling up and down my feed and planning my next money move.

The flaw that I took forever to see in all of my mini gods was the uncertainty that they could ever repay me for my loyalty and dedication. Oftentimes, my repayment was exhaustion. I was empty and, in all honesty, broken. Then like the hypocrite I am, I went to Jehovah God, the one true God, and expected Him to fix everything that I sabotaged during my idolatry. Something so miraculous happened...God restored my mental, physical, and spiritual faith in Him! He permeated my faith so I can be better used in His kingdom.

I was so immature to trust tangible people and things more than Him. I believe I did that because as I was hurting and knowing God had the power to prevent the hurt, I blamed Him for it. That blame game weakened my faith over time. But after building trust again through prayer and confession, my faith was restored. He also gave me the ability to forgive myself for putting other things and people before Him. Even after my transgressions, He still had open arms for me. Loving God comes with a certainty that I could not get from anyone else. God comes with wholeness and completion and that can never be found in the world.

1 KINGS 18: 18-21 NKJV

"And he answered, 'I have not troubled Israel, but you and your father's house have, in that you have forsaken the commandments of the LORD and have followed the Baals. Now therefore, send and gather all Israel to me on Mount Carmel, the four hundred and fifty prophets of Baal, and the four hundred prophets of Asherah, who eat at Jezebel's table.' So Ahab sent for all the children of Israel, and gathered the prophets together on Mount Carmel. And Elijah came to all the people, and said, 'How long will you falter between two opinions? If the LORD is God, follow Him; but if Baal, follow him.' But the people answered him not a word."

PRAYER

Father God, I love you with all of my heart, my soul, and everything that's within me. In my carnal nature, I've chosen things and people of this world over you. Please forgive my transgressions. I will prioritize my time with You and restore my relationship with You. You are the head and source of my life. I shall not put any god before You. In Jesus' name, amen.

CLEANSING THOUGHT

God is first. Period. Don't shoot the messenger. This is His show and we just run around in it. We should happily place God first in our lives and be cautious not to create idle gods during our journey. It's tempting especially because our flesh is weak and we are carnal by nature. If we look back over our lives and see how many times God has kept us, forgiven us, overlooked our faults, and still remains the same...it's a no brainer. Putting God first also gives us the best protection from things and people not meant for us. If we choose other quasi-gods instead, it leaves us open and vulnerable for an attack from the enemy simply because quasi-gods don't possess all power. Assess your life carefully and be sure that you don't make the same mistakes I have made. If you have, luckily Jehovah God, our one true God, believes in second, third, and fourth chances. As long as your heart is pure, He can use it.

1. List some of your favorite things and people. How much time do you spend on these things? Compare this to the time you spend with God.

2. Are you willing to worship God instead of your quasi gods? List your commitments below. Post them somewhere visible daily in order to be intentional about worshipping God and not quasi gods.

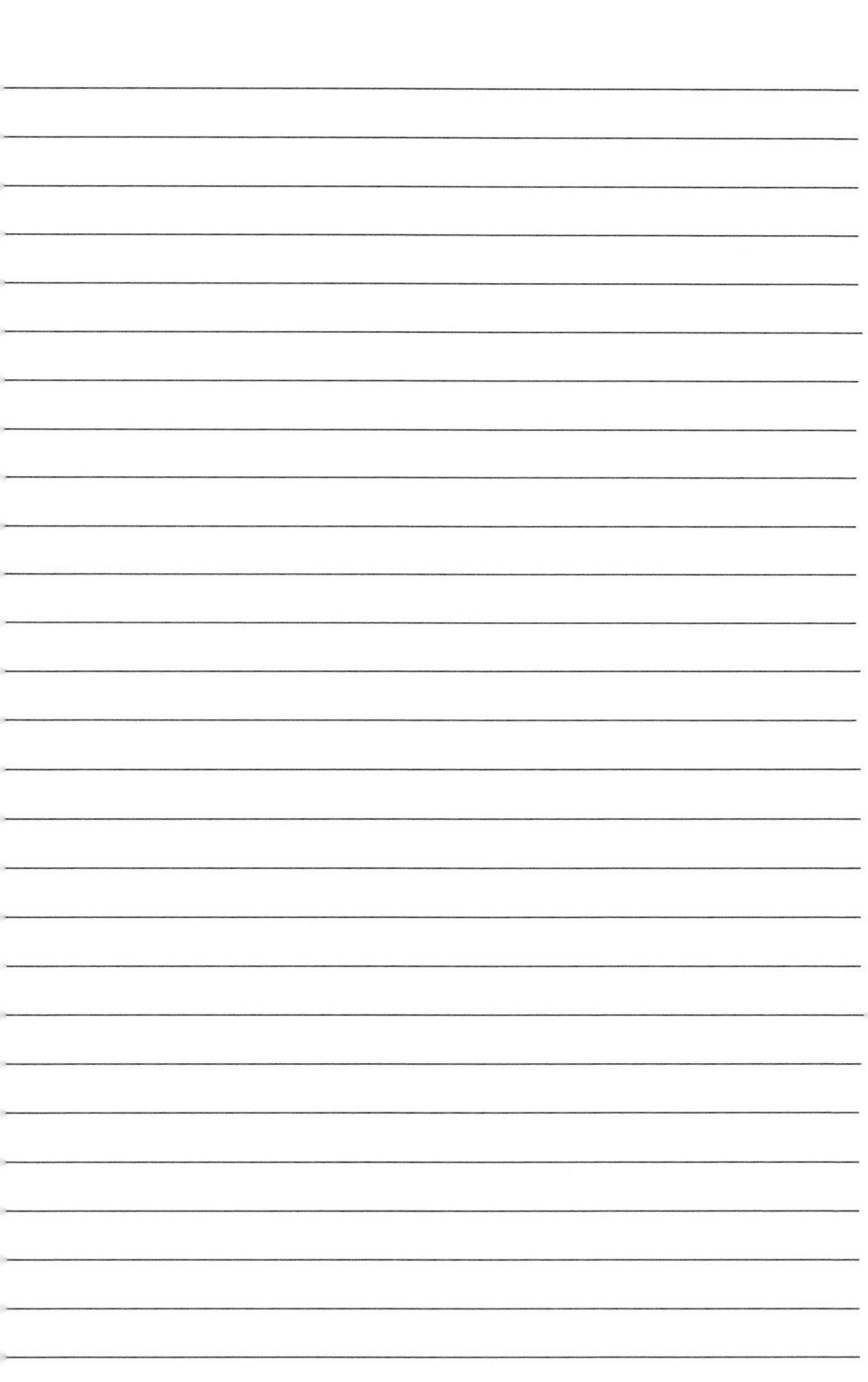

7

N atural disasters blow my mind. In a world oversaturated by technology, God still makes Himself known by creating hurricanes, floods, thunderstorms, tornadoes, and earthquakes just to name a few. These storms come raging in with little warning and put all of our plans and technology to shame. A simple YouTube search can show you how a tornado can rip up an entire block in a matter of minutes. The same can be said for hurricanes and floods that have become mainstream topics and mentioned in popular songs because of their impact; wiping out communities with no warning. I'm sure the people that have been affected by natural disasters thought they were prepared. They watched the news and were told to prep in some form or fashion. They made sure they had some type of collateral to spend in case of an emergency. The stores became barren once the word spread that a storm was approaching. People come from far and wide to purchase water, nonperishable food items, and sources of fire and electricity. All the preparation does not equip them for the damage that some of these storms can produce. If the storm wants to wreak havoc that's exactly what it is going to do.

All of those supplies and plans are comparable to the false sense of protection we have when we are enduring spiritual warfare.

I'm not saying these supplies and plans are not essential, but the only way to accurately prepare yourself for destruction is to know all of the details and capacity it possesses. Just like God assigns angels to do His work, the enemy assigns demons to do the same. To approach our personal storms and struggles in life by our hand alone would be the equivalent of bringing a BB gun to a shootout.

There have been times when I thought I was saved enough to not pray daily or read the Word of God regularly. I really believed I did enough work for God to just coast through life without running into any problems, at least ones that I couldn't fix myself. I had everything a woman could want and cheerleaders around to remind me of how good I was. I armed myself with worldly possessions and ambition and like a thief in the night, the enemy sent roadblocks, torment, confusion, and discord. I didn't have the power to handle those problems by myself. All of the nuggets I collected thus far were helpful but were false senses of protection. The only true source of protection for me was our all-knowing and powerful God. It wasn't until I got back with His program that I was able to navigate the storms that wanted to kill me. We have to allow God to protect us because He knows the magnitude of every storm that comes our way and wants the glory for defeating them.

EPHESIANS 6:11-18 NIV

"Put on the full armor of God, so that you can take your stand against the devil's schemes. For our struggle is not against flesh and blood, but against the rulers, against the authorities, against the powers of this dark world and against the spiritual forces of evil in the heavenly realms. Therefore put on the full armor of God, so that when the day of evil comes, you may be able to stand your ground, and after you have done everything, to stand.

Stand firm then, with the belt of truth buckled around your waist, with the breastplate of righteousness in place, and with your feet fitted with the readiness that comes from the gospel of peace. In addition to all this, take up the shield of faith, with which you can extinguish all the flaming arrows of the evil one. Take the helmet of salvation and the sword of the Spirit, which is the word of God. And pray in the Spirit on all occasions with all kinds of prayers and requests. With this in mind, be alert and always keep on praying for all the Lord's people."

PRAYER

Dear God, my protector from all things, please forgive me for my carnal ways. I am so worldly to think that people and things are in control. You are storm proof and I need You to protect me. I rebuke false senses of protection that dress up like You but lack your power and intention for my life. I rebuke the enemy and his agenda to separate me from you. You are my solid ground, not money, not a warm body, not popularity or status. Lord walk with me as I brave this harsh, destructive world. I love You, trust You and praise Your name, In Jesus' name, amen.

CLEANSING THOUGHT

We must arm ourselves in the Lord daily. The enemy stays on the prowl. He sends imposters and posers to mimic God and it's up to us to weed out the fakes. Short term satisfaction is not protection. If you can't tell the difference, keep praying for discernment. The wisdom of knowing that God is all powerful brings a peace like no other.

1. Are you familiar with the whole armor of God? Find them and list them.
2. What will your spiritual armor protect you from? List it and declare it in Jesus' name.

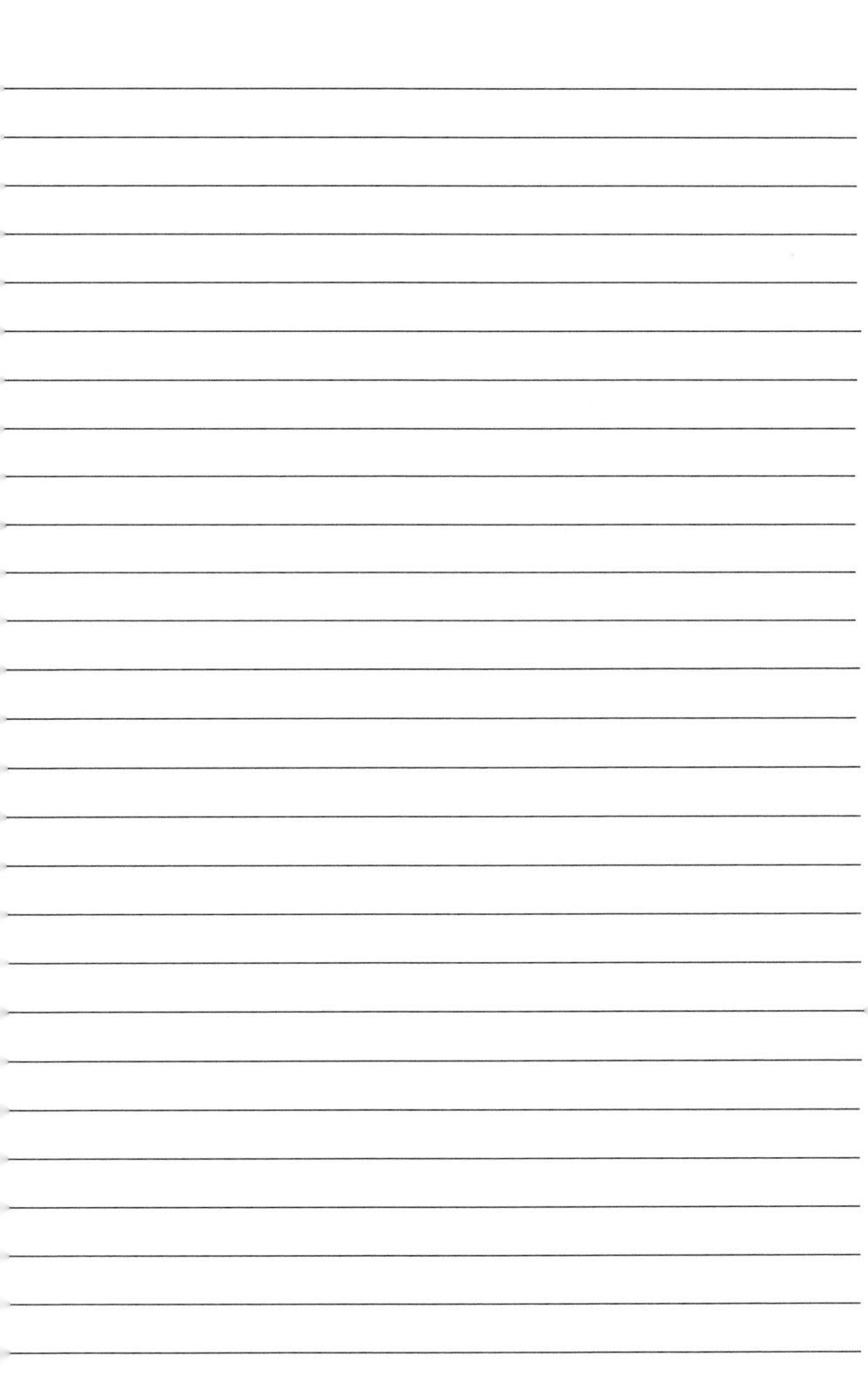

8

BUT CAN YOU SEND ANOTHER SIGN? -SAVED HOT MESS - OK GOD...

This chapter was almost named, "The Making of My Soft Bottom." We've all heard the saying of what a hard head makes...Instead, I decided to be super transparent and quote a prayer that I send to heaven often. I have prayed to God for signs and direction when I've felt that I've reached a fork in the road or when I've been vulnerable to make the wrong decision. I'll give some examples even though I know you already feel me.

"God, can you send me a sign if this man is the one?"

"God, is this job meant for me? If so, send a sign."

"God, is it okay to spend money on this? If not, please send me a sign."

"God, am I putting myself in a bad situation? If so, could you please send me a sign?"

Like clockwork, God would send me signs; subtle or grand, that gave me clarity on how I should move. But like the hardheaded, soft-bottomed Christian that I am, I ignore the sign and then have the audacity to ask God for another one. It's almost as if I am accusing God of making a mistake; like He sent me someone else's sign. It's comical and disobedient at the same time. It's comical because I do it over and over as if the answer will magically change. The truth is that God is not a three-wish genie waiting for me to make requests. He is my maker with my life in His hands. Even though my anxiety-ridden mind frame believes I'm in control, the reality is I am not. The plans I make for myself are always in vain if I don't include God in them. But it gets deeper.

So I ask God for signs, He sends them, I ask for more, He sends more just for me to still do what I feel like doing. Then I have the audacity to get upset and question His love for me after I pretty much inflicted my own demise. It's a disgusting cycle that I am committed to getting out of. As a matter of fact, it's a disgusting cycle that we all will get out of.

First, we must do away with our own ambition. Merriam-Webster defines ambition as "an ardent desire for rank, fame, or power" and "a desire to achieve a particular end." Now in order to have a desire for success, one must first acknowledge what success means. Considering God has an individual purpose for all of us, the only way we can even discover our purpose to succeed in it, is establishing an intimate relationship with Him. Our ambition has to be removed from our carnal interests and repositioned in God. We must be ambitious about our obedience to Him and serving Him, not in order to say we accomplished something in the world. Choosing worldly ambition can leave us high and dry, but choosing to have ambition for God will make room for our spiritual blessings and possibly earthly blessings as well.

Second, if we include God in all of the plans that we make and stay in constant communication with Him, we won't need a specific sign. Our lives will serve as a sign. When we deny God the opportunity to orchestrate our lives we are just as naive as someone who brings sand to the beach. Our relationship with God should be proactive, not reactive. He has already given us the blueprint for walking in our purpose. He also sent His son as insurance for the bumps along the way.

Third, we have to learn to embrace the head bump once we make the wrong decisions. God is omnipresent. If He allows us to experience hardship, it is still with our good in mind. We must learn to skip past the pouting, self-loathing, and begging for more signs. If we truly listen to Him the first time, we can stay on our path of purpose and do so much good in the world. So, let's start thanking God for the signs He already sent before we ask for more.

ISAIAH 7:11-14

"Ask a sign of the Lord your God; let it be deep as Sheol or high as heaven. But Ahaz said, I will not ask, and I will not put the Lord to the test. Then Isaiah[d] said: "Hear then, O house of David! Is it too little for you to weary mortals, that you weary my God also? Therefore the Lord himself will give you a sign. Look, the young woman[e] is with child and shall bear a son, and shall name him Immanuel.""

PRAYER

Eternal God! Thank You for being You. Please forgive me for being unlike You. Please forgive me for not trusting in the instruction You've already provided. Help me to not focus on my will but make Your desires my desires. I have issues with control. It stems from a heart problem. Give me a spiritual heart transplant so I can put my trust in You wholly. I love You and believe You are all powerful to show me the way. In Jesus' name, amen.

CLEANSING THOUGHT

I think we always have that innermost knowledge that God has already answered what we're asking Him for. We are just so antsy to control everything that we deny the truth when it isn't what we want to hear. We have to get connected with God in such a way that we don't even need a sign. That's the standard. When we abandon our own ambitions, seek God first in all we do, and learn to embrace our journey, we won't miss out on His divine signs.

1.　　How has God given you signs?
2.　　List some times you got signs from God but chose not to listen. What was the outcome?

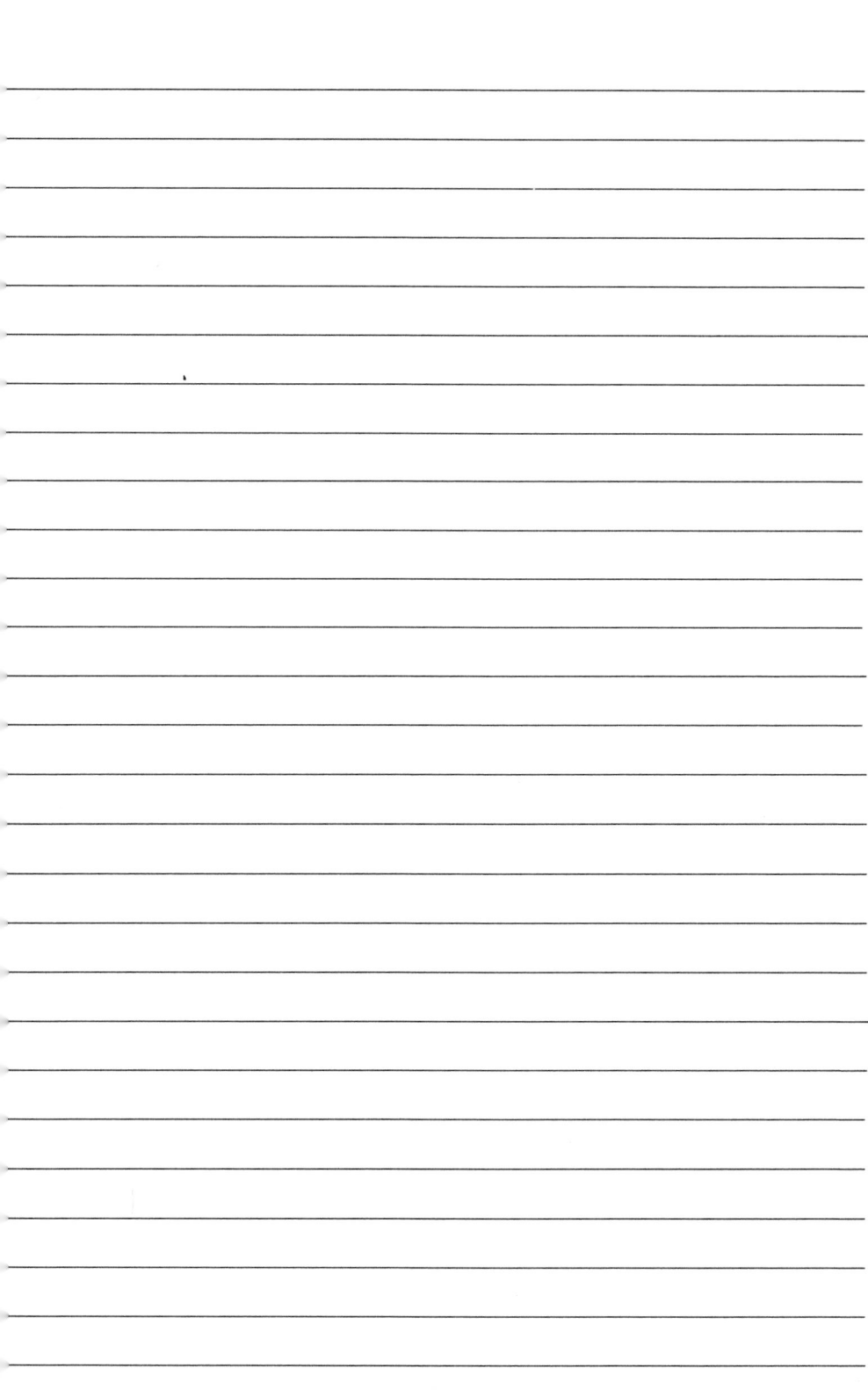

Celebrating others is truly a pastime of mine. I love seeing others be blessed with prosperity and growth. I also understand that some people have an alternative reaction to seeing other people prosper. Envy and jealousy rise up instead of joy. The reason they get jealous is because they see someone else with something that they wish to have. That logic is strange to me because I believe in my heart of hearts that "I can do all things through Christ that strengthen me." If I see someone reach a level or attain something material that I want, all I have to do is pray, work hard, manifest, and it's mine...

However, there is one thing that does stir up jealousy in me; seeing a woman with a loving father. A present father. A father that shares their genetics, face shape, and personality. A father that can recall all of their accomplishments in life off the top of his head. A father that was there to catch her everytime she fell. A physical father that would declare war over anyone that tried to hurt his baby girl. A father that prepared his daughter and taught her the game so even when her heart would be broken one day, she would have the wisdom to weather it. A father that constantly assured his daughter how beautiful she was so she never had to seek the wrong attention from a man. That was something I could not manifest and work hard for.

I wished upon every star, got on my knees and prayed, tried to be on my best behavior and be as loving as humanly possible. No physical father dropped out of the sky for me. My friends shared their fathers sometimes and I even had some male teachers take a paternal role with me, but it wasn't the same. I wasn't theirs for real. They couldn't wipe the tears I cried at night from broken hearts and failure. Nor could they marvel in what they poured into me as I reached various milestones in life. As grateful as I was for the father figures that helped me through life, I still wanted a daddy of my own. So, I found myself envying women that had that. I saw how watered they were. I saw the level of respect they got from the men they dated, because those men knew not to get over on a daddy's girl.

I didn't feel chosen. I felt second best. I felt unworthy, dirty, unlovable, and even less precious. Why did my physical father decide not to fight for me? I even found myself fantasizing about having a dysfunctional, an imperfect father. As long as he was present and loved me, I'd feel more valuable. Something was better than nothing, right? It was only a matter of time before my toxic outlook about my daddy void manifested into unhealthy relationships with men. I had no blueprint on what to expect, so I took lots of disrespect, abuse, and pain from men. Whenever I was mistreated I always found a way to blame myself. I connected my ability to please others to my worthiness of love.

It wasn't until my late twenties that I realized just how much being fatherless had an impact on what I accepted. It even affected my relationship with Christ as I sought salvation. I never practiced what it meant to trust a father and experience unconditional love from a man, so it took some time for me to understand how God viewed me, but praise be to God! He waited on me. God waited until I was so burnt out and disgusted about my misfortune with men and the only option I had was Him. When I was so broken and wanted to die, it was God that lifted my head. When I didn't feel that I was beautiful, He transformed my mind to see myself in a better light. When I needed healthy, physical touch, He encamped me with people that loved to give hugs of assurance. When my money was funny, He orchestrated my finances in a way that I would experience overflow. The father that I yearned for was here all along.

The good news is God is your father, too. He made you and me in His image. He was there for every accomplishment, hiccup, and failure we ever experienced and has no plans to leave. In His word He said if we ask for forgiveness, He keeps no record of our wrongdoing. He loves us unconditionally. He is willing to fight our battles. God has the ability to be all powerful which is something a physical father could never be. It's through Him that we can do anything. Men that abandon their daughters may not understand the long-term damage and pain they cause but that pain is never too much for God. The peace that has entered my life since I've embraced my relationship with my heavenly father is priceless. My daddy blessed me with everything I am and everything I have. This inheritance fully outweighs any void.

PSALM 68:4-6 NIV

"Sing to God, sing in praise of his name, extol him who rides on the clouds[b]; rejoice before him—his name is the Lord. A father to the fatherless, a defender of widows, is God in his holy dwelling. God sets the lonely in families,[c] he leads out the prisoners with singing; but the rebellious live in a sun-scorched land."

MARK 5:34:4 NIV

He said to her, "Daughter, your faith has made you well; go in peace, and be healed of your disease."

PRAYER

Father, You created me in Your image and for that I thank You. I thank You so much for seeing in me what I can't see in myself sometimes. Forgive me for falling short. I get caught up in this world. My biological father is imperfect. He let me down and I've been searching to fill that void for a long time. I declare the search is over! God, You waited for me and I'm here now. I'm Yours. Draw me close to You so that I won't feel another void for anything ever again. I love You. In Jesus' name, amen.

CLEANSING THOUGHT

Fatherlessness is real. It affects people deeply and causes long-lasting pain. God is so loyal and loving that He will meet us where we are if we just allow Him to have a relationship with us. Monetary heirlooms are a blessing but they can't beat being an heir to the most high God. No tears, no depth, no wounds, no trauma, no lies, no truth is too hard for God. Our daddy loves us. So let Him.

---

1. How has fatherlessness affected you or those around you?
2. What do you expect from your heavenly father that a physical father can not do?

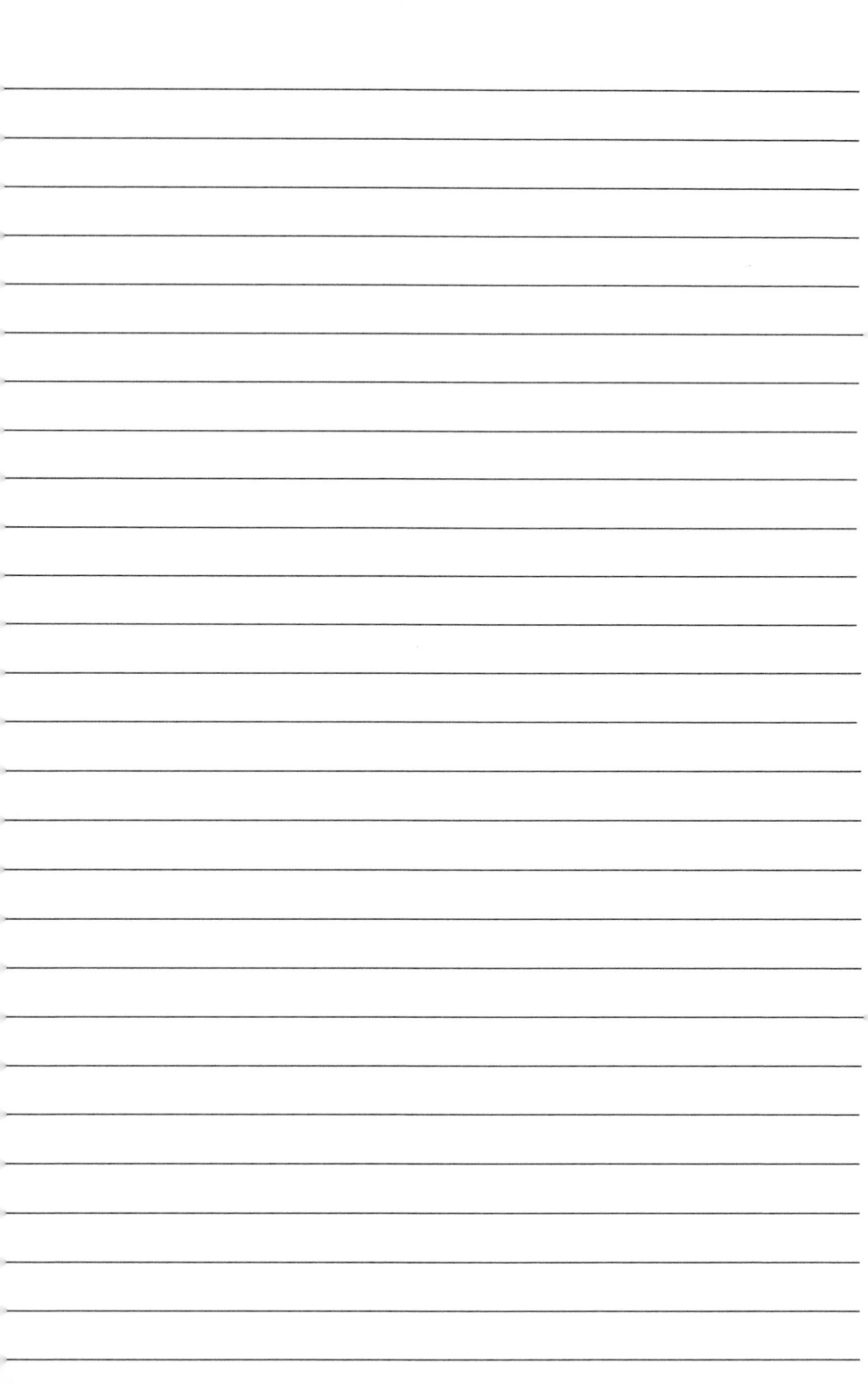

.

10

Most women in our culture have been told at least once, whether in our childhood or adulthood, that our body is our temple and we should cherish it in its natural form. A lot of elders gave this advice as a response to us wanting a cool tattoo or piercing. Little did they know that their advice caused a forbidden thrill. People all over the world use piercings, tattoos, and body modification as an outlet for individualism. One very well known form of body modification is plastic surgery.

According to the American Society of Plastic Surgeons (ASPS), almost 18 million people underwent surgical and/or minimally invasive cosmetic procedures in the United States in 2018. I'm sure every person that braved the thought of getting their first tattoo or piercing was scolded by an overbearing elder that "your body is your temple." Their sentiment is Bible-based indeed and insists that our bodies are perfect the way that they are without any permanent changes. And believe me, that's extremely beautiful. But the risqué reputation that tattoos and piercings earned didn't stand a chance against the decision being made by millions of American.

We are choosing plastic surgery as if it's as simple as choosing what shirt to wear. Based on the shallow nature of our society, looking as close to perfect as possible, it is a desire that even the fear of death can't damper. Ultimately, people have the final say so over what is done to their bodies. That still doesn't stop the finger-wagging elders from condemning those who choose to go under the knife in the name of vanity. While I understand both those for or against body modification, I relate more to someone who will make the choice to get plastic surgery.

You see, this temple that I have is incredibly flawed. My feet are flat, my knocked knees are fat, my butt isn't as big as I'd like it to be but my thighs and stomach surely make up for it in size, my breasts sag, my stretch marks are uncountable, and my bottom teeth are crooked.

I remember when my mother harmlessly introduced shapewear into my life. I was about 14 years old and although I had already understood the confinement of wearing bras for my large to scale breasts, I didn't understand the purpose behind shapewear. I had to wear a formal dress and definitely had some love handles (mostly baby fat). My mother's advice to me was to wear the shapewear under my clothing so that I would look smooth, presentable and well-kept. I know she meant well, and I'm grateful for her guidance, but I wondered if my leaner friends had to wear a tight and confining item under their clothes to "look presentable". I began to obsess over bodies and people that were naturally "presentable" and developed an unhealthy perception about my body. I felt unworthy and would blame any mishap that I faced in life, on my imperfect body. To this day, I am ashamed to admit, I still have unhealthy perceptions about my body.

Seeing the impact that a small waist, Brazilian butt, perky boobs, and perfect teeth have on society definitely reroutes the idea that a natural body is just as good. The reality is that none of us asked for the bodies that God blessed us with nor did we ask for the social norms that deem our bodies socially acceptable or not. It's frustrating to not feel good enough, pretty enough, or bold enough living in a world that feels like an uphill battle. I believe we fail most in the area of being grateful for a body...period. We are not guaranteed working limbs, health, or strength. And the functions of the body parts that we usually choose to alter have no correlation to the way we enhance them by surgery. With all due respect, a larger butt does nothing but stink. Instead of being so critical of our flaws, we really should embrace our bodies as they are. We also have to be careful of what and who we let inside of our bodies. I remember a long time ago a wise man told me that my eyes, ears, mouth and womb were all ways that energy can enter my body. He cautioned me to be careful what I look at, listen to, say, and what type of person I choose to share my body with. Once certain energy invades your body, its hard for it to be removed. A temple is a sacred place that can serve as an extension of your works, talent and ability to prosper. You must be grateful for it though. We only get one.

PSALM 139:13-14

"For You formed my inward parts; You covered me in my mother's womb. I will praise You, for I am fearfully and wonderfully made; Marvelous are Your works, And that my soul knows very well."

PRAYER

Holy One, God of everything, thank You for my body. You had me in mind when you formed me. Somehow after seeing certain images and societal norms I have lost sight of my natural beauty. I've created a standard in my mind of how my body should look. I'm ashamed of my vanity and I give it to you. Please reset my expectation for my body to gratefulness. Help me to take care of my body by eating healthy and exercising. Help me appreciate and nurture the beauty that you gave me. Help me to appreciate my unique physical appearance and have a degree of self love that honors you. In Jesus' name, amen.

CLEANSING THOUGHT

This is probably one of my top 3 areas of opportunity. I struggle with having a positive body image. I have conformed to the world's standard of beauty and it robs me of my self worth. That's why we have to start giving this issue to God as well. If we can't thank Him for what we do have, ask Him for the strength to safely transform our outer body to match the inner beauty. We've been programmed to think God is so uppity that He doesn't care about our insecurities. He cares about every single thing about us. We just have to show our faith by bringing it to Him.

---

1. List what you consider to be your body flaws. For every flaw, list something you love about your body.
2. Are you caring for your body to the best of your ability?

11

"**H**ardships often prepare ordinary people for an extraordinary destiny," C.S. Lewis once said. Quotes like this are both beautifully accurate and bittersweet. This is the realization that true happiness comes with a price. Considering Jesus paid the ultimate price so smoothly, (thanks JC), we should be the last to complain when we don't get our way. Have you ever complained about something so deeply and for so long that you made yourself feel childish and ungrateful? There have been times where I have allowed comparison; the thief of joy, to make me feel as if I had nothing and was worth nothing. I would wonder why I had to experience certain hardships and others didn't. I would even wonder if I was born into the wrong family. I would convince myself that whatever difficulty I faced was ultimately my fault and self-loathing became a natural response to any adversity. I was the queen of pity parties until my ungrateful butt had to see children living with cancer or limited mobility, mothers who couldn't feed their children, or veterans who had no place to lay their head at night.

Someone always has it worse off than you. The assumption that bad things are only happening to you or that you don't deserve to go through anything is unfortunately a side effect of the pretentious nature we have adapted. Repeat after me, "NOBODY OWES ME ANYTHING!" God's grace is so sufficient, I believe it spoils us. Just like a child that was given too much and didn't deserve it grows up to be pretentious and ungrateful...we are guilty. It's not too late for us though. Start asking yourself in the midst of hard situations if you view it as glass half empty or glass half full? Gratefulness is the best anecdote for an ungrateful spirit. Always remember; practice makes perfect. We must make an effort and incorporate the habit of gratefulness into our everyday lives so it becomes second nature. I can imagine that God can relate to the same frustration I have when my children are ungrateful after I bust my butt. He gave His only begotten son so that we could live. That alone should brighten up our day. When we focus on what we have, there is no room to worry about what we think is lacking.

II TIMOTHY 3:1-5

"But know this, that in the last days perilous times will come: For men will be lovers of themselves, lovers of money, boasters, proud, blasphemers, disobedient to parents, unthankful, unholy, unloving, unforgiving, slanderers, without self-control, brutal, despisers of good, traitors, headstrong, haughty, lovers of pleasure rather than lovers of God, having a form of godliness but denying its power. And from such people turn away!"

PRAYER

Heavenly Father, thank You so much for another day and another chance. Forgive me for my carnal ways and actions. My ungratefulness has blocked my own blessings. There have been dangers seen and unseen that You have saved me from. You've held my destiny in Your hands and protected me when no one else could. I want to have childlike joy again. I want to appreciate each moment of light and darkness and know that it is for my good. In Jesus' name, amen.

CLEANSING THOUGHT

Entitlement is such an awful spirit. We can no longer subscribe to the idea that we are owed everything but understand that everything we have is a blessing. We must not compare, for it is the thief of joy. Being ungrateful and entitled is a prideful way to live. As they say, pride comes before the fall. So, let's save the head bump and start being more mindful of our privileges.

1.   What does the Bible say about ungratefulness?
2.   How do you feel when someone is ungrateful for something you've done for them?

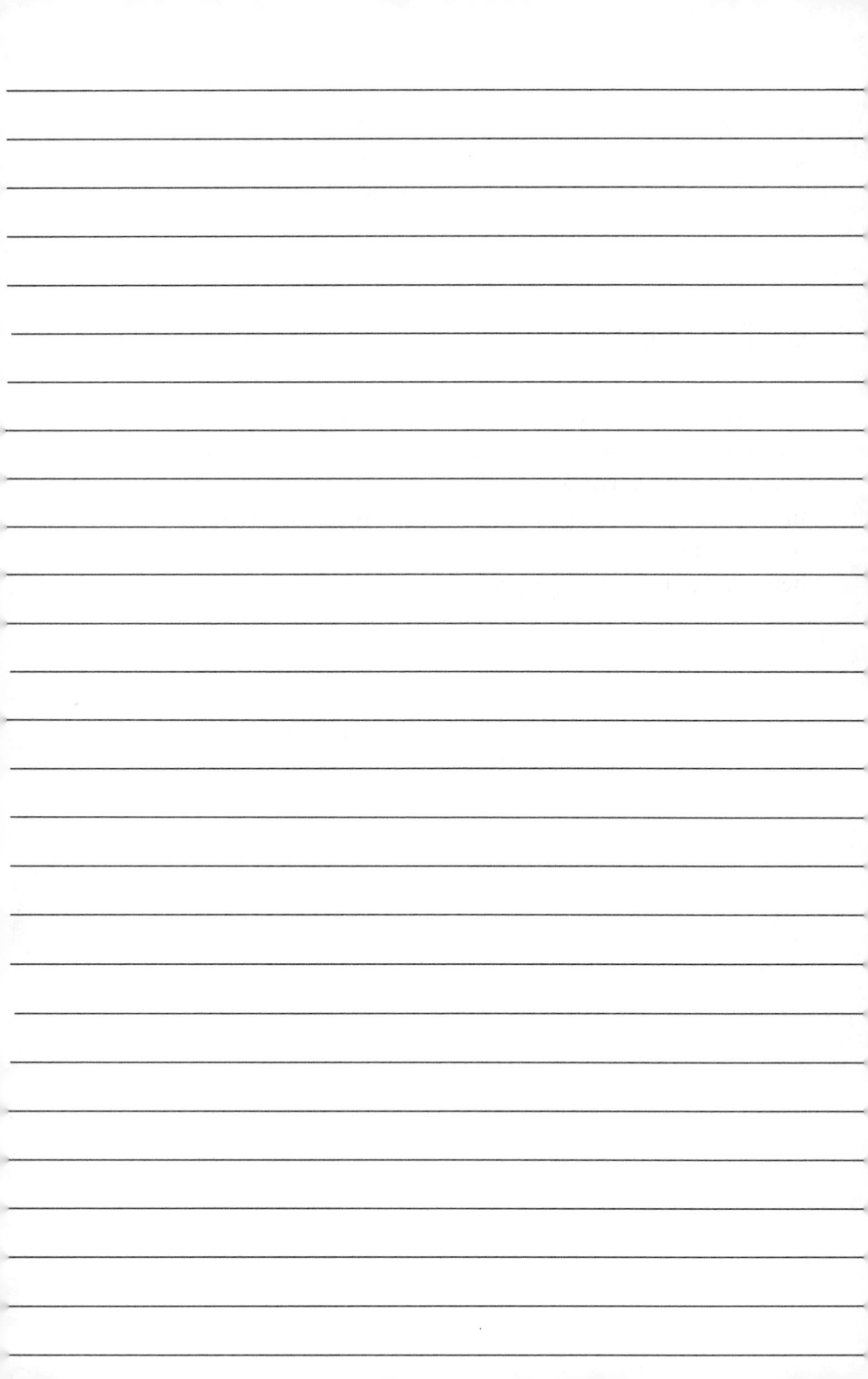

12

Whether it's a flute, glass, mug, or cup, there's nothing like a crowd of people coming together to agree or declare during a toast. The preferred beverage is usually some type of libation and it's usually done with joy, excitement, or emotion. I think a topic that some Christians avoid is indulgence. We believe that since we work so hard to do the right thing that it's only fair that we are allowed the opportunity to indulge sometimes.

My indulgence of choice is a beautiful, timeless, and available glass of wine. My favorite is a tie between a cold moscato or a room temperature, flavorful red. The buds of my tongue are tingling just thinking about it. But just like with anything else, it's not a good idea to have too much of a good thing. The Bible proclaims wine to be good but still instructs us to not have "too much" wine (1 Timothy 3:8). We have to consider our intent when enjoying different things and experiences. The sad part is I tend to turn towards my indulgences most when I'm going through something or unknowingly looking for a substitute for God. I'm usually looking for something or someone that's going to make my life easier or at least make it appear that way. For example, as a mother, I have to be present and aware at all times.

I can't clock out of motherhood but I can be present in an altered state.

A lot of people use alcohol, some people use other substances, and some people use work. Whatever your indulgence is, use it sparingly but not as a substitute for God. I understand how frustrating life can be. We often search for a tangible solution to our pain. It's almost like an itch that needs scratching. However, too much scratching leads to tearing. For that reason, I have to watch how much I drink. Being predisposed to addiction on both sides of my family, alcoholism could creep in. Alcoholism is more acceptable by society and harder to diagnose than other addictions just because of how normalized it is. We often boast, "Jesus made wine" but not as a celebration or glorifying His wonder. We say it defensively to excuse our over indulgence. I'm challenging you and myself to be mindful of overindulgence. Make room for God to fill our voids instead of temporary satisfactions. I'm certain He won't disappoint. He never does. So cheers to lifting up our hands more than we lift up our cups.

EPHESIANS 5:15-18 NIV

"Be very careful, then, how you live—not as unwise but as wise, making the most of every opportunity, because the days are evil. Therefore do not be foolish, but understand what the Lord's will is. Do not get drunk on wine, which leads to debauchery. Instead, be filled with the Spirit."

PRAYER

Dear God,

Thank you for being my Heavenly Father and blessing me with your Holy Spirit. Forgive me for falling temptation to my flesh. When I go through various obstacles and need a release, I sometimes turn to drinking or other vices. It's a temporary fix and my obsession for a worldly release takes up space I could use to get closer to you. I believe in You to be all that I need. Everything else is extra, but unnecessary. Convict me to make better decisions and trust You more than my vices. In Jesus' name, amen.

CLEANSING THOUGHT

We are not blaming it on the alcohol no more! God made wine and He made it well, but He never made it to be a substitute for Him. He gave us an inch by saying we can have some wine. Let's not take a mile. Our effort to be obedient is worth a lot.

1.   What are your vices? Addiction(s)? Identify the root cause of these in your life.
2.   Can you celebrate without a vice? Why or why not?

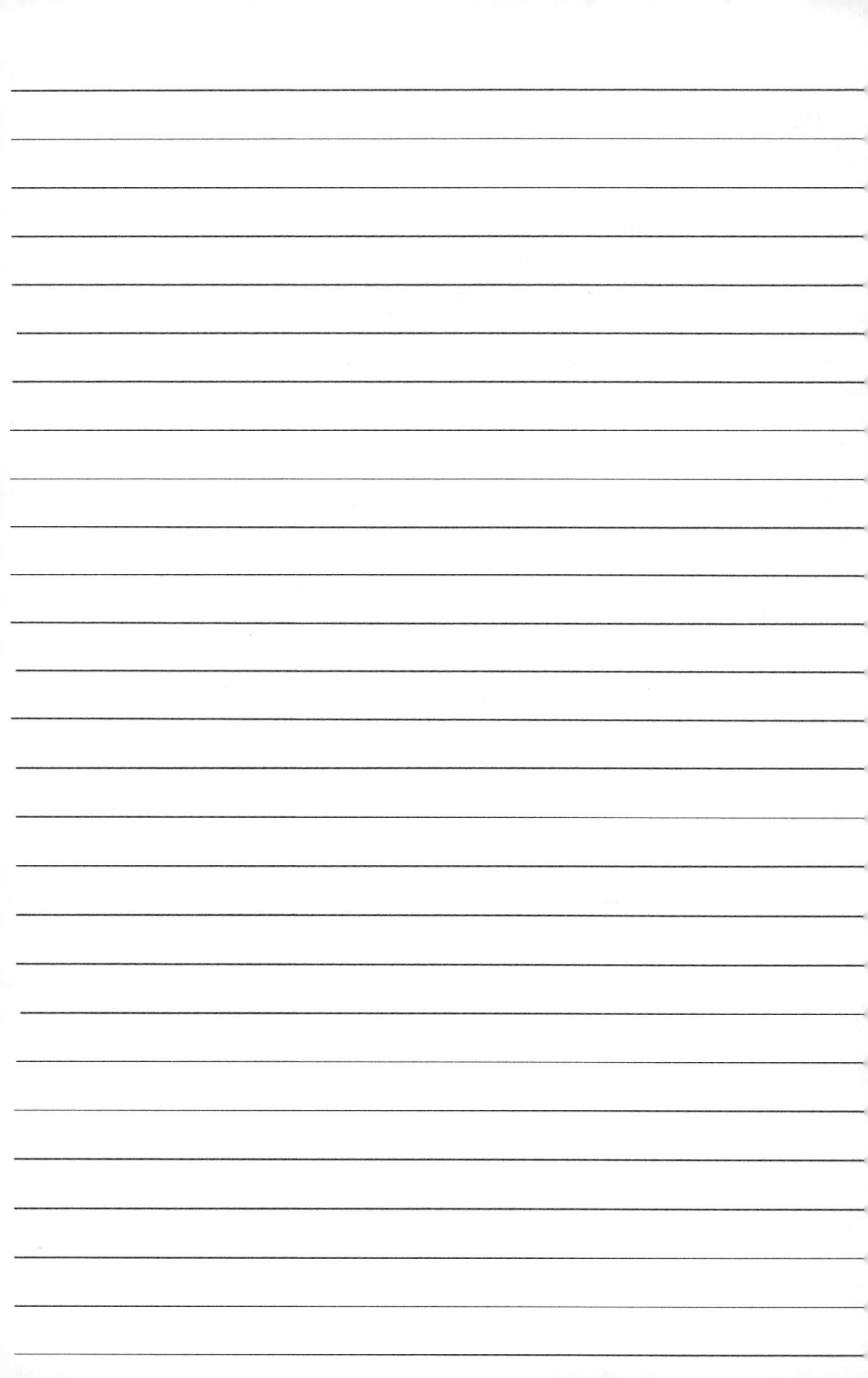

SOFT-SAVED HOT MESS-DRIP TOO

13

"**D**on't dim your light to make others comfortable" is the advice my mama tried to give me. By the time she told me this I had already fallen into the pattern of hiding my attractive qualities to make those around me not feel less than. In my warped reality I was doing them a favor. I can go all the way back to the first time I was told that I talked like a white girl. (By the way can we please leave that behind? It's so damaging to black girls.) At a young age I had a large vocabulary and was encouraged to speak proper English so that I could master it before I adapted slang. Telling me that speaking correctly separated me from my race made me wonder what I could do to solidify my blackness. So, I studied my peers, their slang, and patterns so I, too, could be more black. I'm ashamed to say I purposely spoke incorrectly sometimes just so I could fit in. It was ignorant but I wanted to belong.

I took this horrible habit into adulthood. I dimmed my light for boyfriends, co-workers, friends, and even family members. My false need to be accepted went against my dreams of excellence because in order to get into the rooms I wanted to be in, I needed to stand out and be unique. I remember the first time I heard the song "Drip too hard" by Lil Baby. The song is about the ultimate flex. Overnight, the word "drip" went from something that came out of a faucet to a whole movement that included showing

65

yourself to the world in the best light. Droplet emojis meant even more than heart emojis. Oh, how I wanted to "Drip too hard." I wanted to be so proud of myself and let my light shine like others did, but all I could do was drip too soft. I was more comfortable with others shining.

One day, I came to the realization that I was also making a spiritual mistake. If God had placed certain gifts and talents in me, who am I to hide them? I can't put what I think is best for people above God's plan for my life. I also had to ask myself what kind of family and friends would resent me for being great? Was that even healthy and/or acceptable? No, it's not.

People that are negative and envious have a personal problem and we should never conform to them but maintain what God has deemed true. He is the orchestrator and if He wanted everyone to be creative, He would've given that gift to everyone. We have to stop leaning on our own understanding and seeing the world from such a small view. We have to have the confidence of God and be proud of the light He gave us. I think that's what Harry Dixon Loes, well-known Christian hymn writer, had on his mind when he wrote, "This Little Light of Mine." We all should sing this song as adults because it hits a lot different now. The confidence in God is the cure for drippin' too soft. Even if we cannot stand on our own confidence we have to find the strength to stand on His.

2 CORINTHIANS 3:11 NKJV

"For if what is passing away was glorious, what remains is much more glorious. Therefore, since we have such hope, we use great boldness of speech—"

PRAYER

Omnipresent God, thank You for Your grace as I find my way. Please forgive me for not walking in the authority that You gave me. I can't recall it but You know the moment in time that my self-esteem was tarnished. You know what experience caused me to alter my level of confidence. You are the fixer. Fix me, God. Help me to be more confident in You so I can speak up and speak out for Your kingdom. I need Your confidence in me to fulfill my purpose. I want to be more like You. In Jesus' name, amen.

CLEANSING THOUGHT

Many of our heads are bowed due to insecurity, shame, or just miseducation about who we are. We are a part of a royal priesthood. We are children of the King. Lord knows the enemy has an army that is bold and ready. He cannot cancel our gifts, but he can cancel our confidence in them. We owe it to God to lift up our heads and walk in the authority that He gave to us. Our lights are meant to shine. The world did not give it and cannot take it away.

1. When was the first time you can recall dimming your light to make someone more comfortable?
2. What is your definition of humbleness? How does humbleness affect your self esteem?

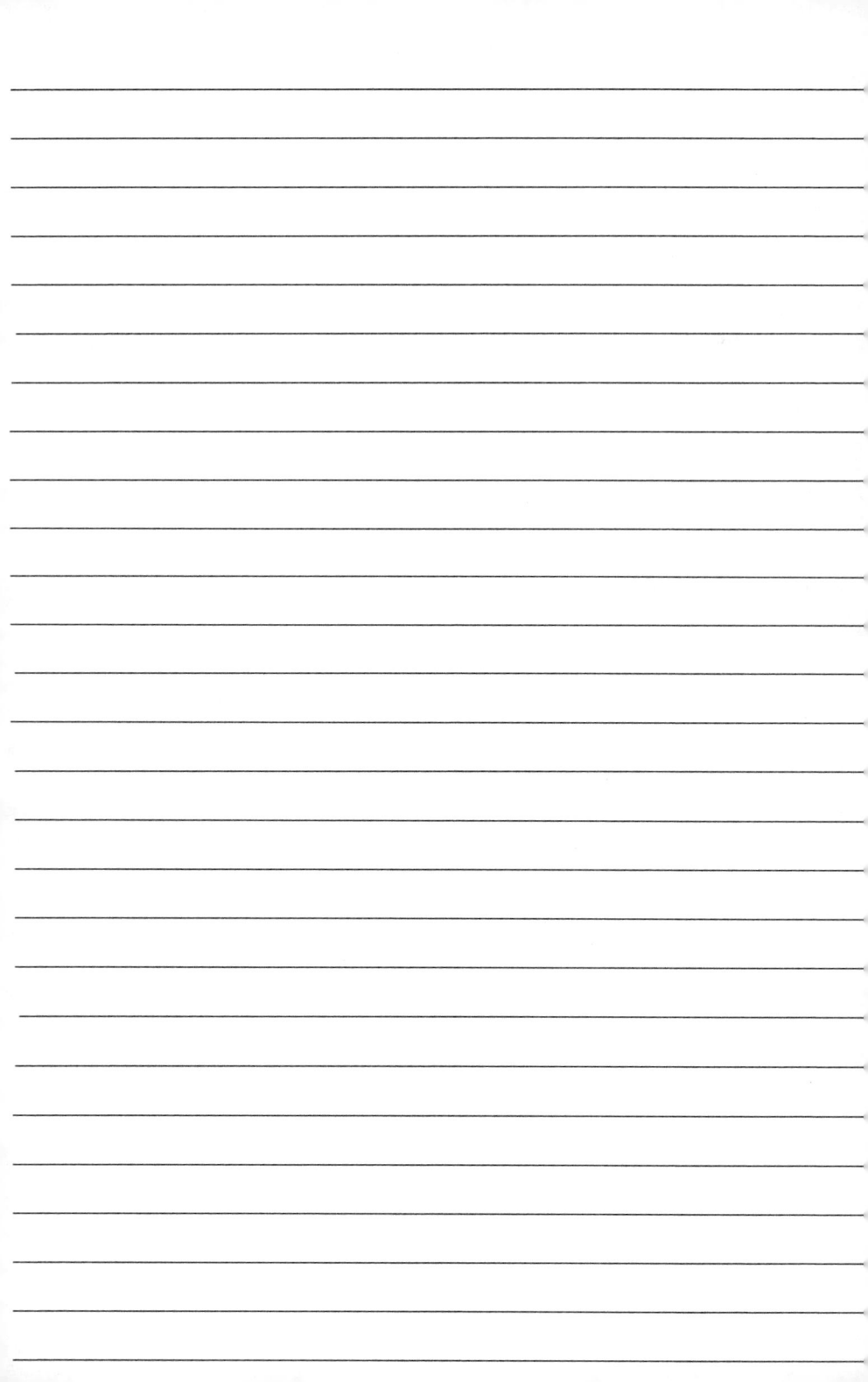

14

How many of you have given the side eye when you've heard someone claim that God "told them something" when it comes to material things? *raises hand*

I think the skeptical response is because God is so omniscient and for Him to go out of His way to deliver a message to us for small vanities just seems iffy. Some people give God credit only to solidify it or disarm any attempt to disagree. Someone could easily manipulate a situation by declaring that God said it. While I question the authenticity of someone that tells me this just to try to sway my response, I do believe in God sending signs. The Bible is full of moments in time where He has sent signs and wonders.

I've received divine green lights from God that have been the starting point for businesses, prevented tragedies from happening, and catapulted me on the path of my destiny. All good things come with instructions. In order to hear God's directions, I have to make sure I'm in the proper position to receive what He's saying. I have to distinguish His voice from the noise. I have to know when it's really God. I have to back away from the world.

One specific time where God gave me a divine green light was to get a job. As mediocre as that sounds, let me give you the backstory. So outside of being a published author, I'm a licensed esthetician and celebrity makeup artist. I proudly own and operate my business. The autonomy of entrepreneurship is one of the best perks while also being a mother. There's a freedom in making your own schedule and working your own hours and the last thing an entrepreneur wants to do again is clock in to a job. My pride had to move when I decided to leave my husband at the dusk of a global pandemic. The opportunity presented itself for me to take on a job as a library aide. I took the job listening to God's divine green light. When my city was forced into quarantine and I wasn't able to take clients for my business, I was distraught. But God knew that I would need that job to sustain my children and me during such a misfortunate time. If I would have let the sin of pride get in the way of God's direction, I wouldn't have had the safety net that I have had.

Sin is what keeps us from God. Where sin is heavy, God's invitation is blocked. The biggest ideas I've ever had came from fasting and praying, just like His word says. I can get a daily affirmation app, I can put up color coordinated post-its on my mirror, and manifest all I want, but those things are in vain if I don't fast and pray. My green lights should always be aligned with God's plan to get in accordance with His plans for me. All of us have a plan or path that was divinely created just for us. We have to place our desires and flesh to the side in order to hear our spiritual GPS; God's Path for Saints.

ISAIAH 30:18-21

"Therefore the Lord waits to be gracious to you, and therefore he exalts himself to show mercy to you. For the Lord is a God of justice; blessed are all those who wait for him. For a people shall dwell in Zion, in Jerusalem; you shall weep no more. He will surely be gracious to you at the sound of your cry. As soon as he hears it, he answers you. And though the Lord give you the bread of adversity and the water of affliction, yet your Teacher will not hide himself anymore, but your eyes shall see your Teacher. And your ears shall hear a word behind you, saying, "This is the way, walk in it," when you turn to the right or when you turn to the left."

PRAYER

Dear God, thank You for leading me this far in my life. Thank You for keeping me out of harm's way. Thank You for the things that never happened that could have. Forgive me for being a know-it-all and sabotaging Your navigation for me. I want to make the right choices and decisions when I am faced with forks in the road. Deliver me from spirits of desperation. I've never seen the righteous forsaken so please continue to hold my hand as I try to live righteously. Help me weed out the voices that aren't Yours. Father, take the wheel. Help me to move out of the way. You tell me to go, I will. I trust You and I know You have my best in mind, all the time. In Jesus' name, amen.

CLEANSING THOUGHT

As fun as sin seems, it keeps us from God's direction for us. We can't hear God clearly if we let too many voices into our hearts and minds. We are never waiting on God, He's ready. He waits on us because He loves us. He also loves His plans for us and if we aren't obedient to listen to Him, He'll get the outcome He wants with or without our cooperation. It's in our best interest to let our creator give us the green light so we can give Him the glory in the end.

1. Name a time when God placed a ram in the bush for you?
2. When you say yes to God, what are you sometimes saying no to?

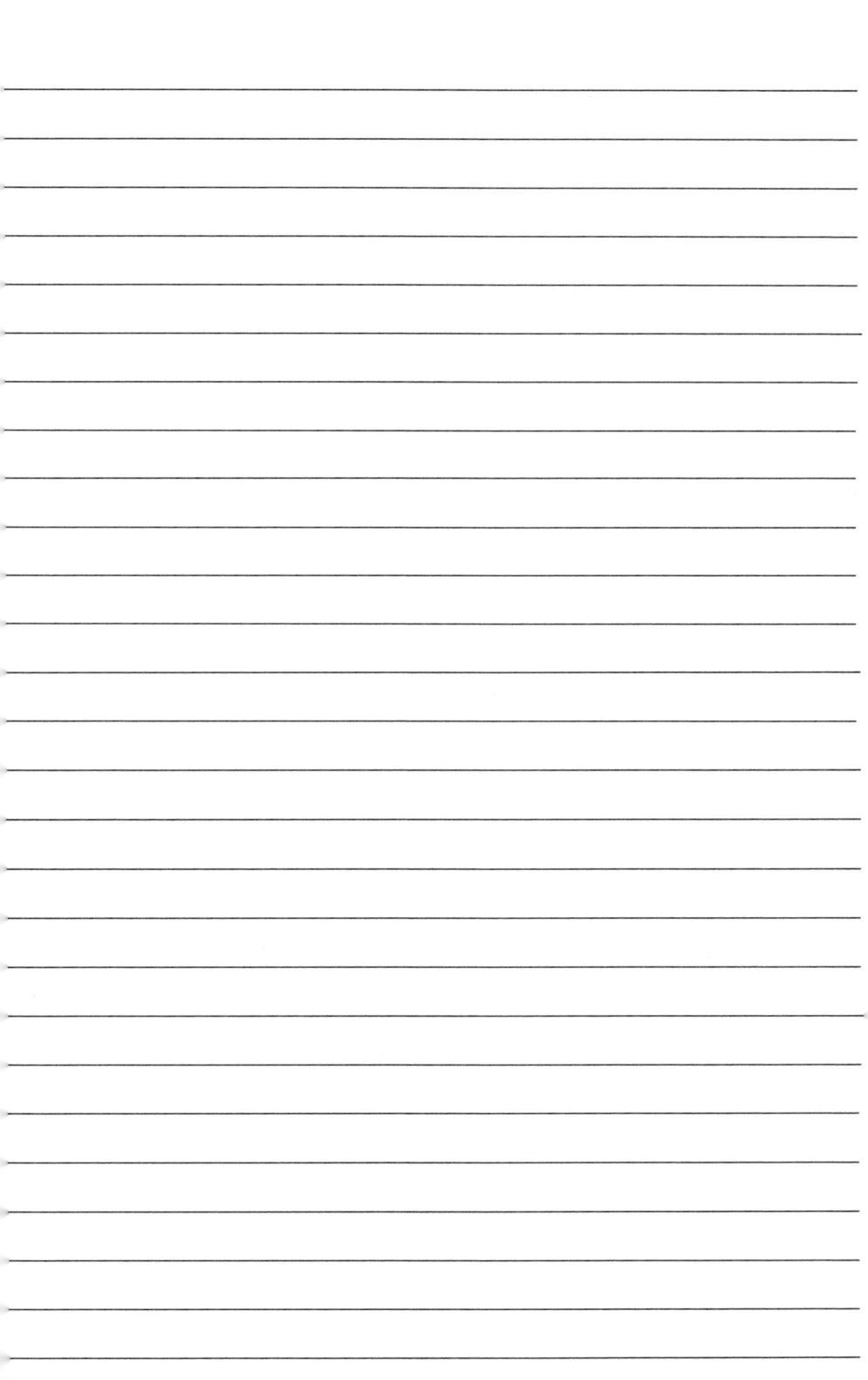

15

In the film, Selena, we saw one of the most savage displays of betrayal. When Selena's friend and president of her fan club, Yolanda, was confronted about stealing, her instinctual solution was to kill Selena. It showed us first hand how an emotion can be born as jealousy but turn into death. The root of jealousy is fear. The fear of Selena being talented, sought-after, loved, adored, and yet to reach her peak was strong in Yolanda's spirit. It festered in her, gave her negative thoughts and ate her from the inside out, just because it wasn't her. I'm sure the question often graced her conscious, "Why her?" It is because of that depiction that I condemn that question. It is a toxic reaction that so many of us ask when we don't feel picked, pretty enough, or worthy enough of things we want. It's a question that a lot of us can't actually handle the truth of.

To envy someone else is in vain simply because we don't know what it's like to even be in that person's shoes. The hard work, long nights, hunger, isolation, mental anguish, and rejection that a person faces to become a boss is usually buried in their past. Yet they are envied for tangible things that can't compare to the price they paid to be in a position to be envied by anyone. It's a vicious cycle that has put a wrench in families, friendships, and even marriages. One thing is for certain, the spirit of "why her" is not something a follower of God should have. If God chooses to bless anyone, who are we to question that? How dare we turn something divinely placed into a meaningless competition? Perhaps God allows us to see others be blessed to show His power. Maybe God let's us witness other's blessings to teach us how to be humble and gracious. He was clear when He said, "You have not because you ask not." Whatever His prerogative is, it's not ours to judge.

Before I seem like I'm bashing those who haven't been dealt the best hands in life, let me shine a light on the type of heart that can fall prey to this spirit. If you can dig deep enough with me about these hard topics, we can really start a healing process that will bless us all generationally. I've noticed that a lot of jealousy and envy is taught. There are mother's that raised their children with resentment in their hearts so they grew jealous of their own children. There are families that have participated in favoritism and the victims in those families turned to that thinking as a coping mechanism because they never thought they could become the favorite. Colorism, trauma, abuse, poverty or any other low vibrating painful experience can all be a breeding ground for "murderous level jealousy".

Anyone who carries around a bitterness for never getting a break or getting picked or just being loved correctly has my sympathy. I apologize on their behalf. But the reaction should never be to sabotage another. Maybe the energy used to hate another person for navigating life well should be placed into something positive. And believe me, practice makes perfect. If you see a woman dressed nicely who took the time to style her hair, put on a little makeup and select a nice outfit, wish her well. If it doesn't hurt, give her a compliment. Celebrate her instead of asking why things are looking good for her. I once heard an elder say, "When you get to witness someone receive a blessing, be happy. Because if you're close enough to see it, some of that blessing will spill over on you."

JAMES 3:13-18 NKJV

"Who is wise and understanding among you? Let him show by good conduct that his works are done in the meekness of wisdom. But if you have bitter envy and self-seeking in your hearts, do not boast and lie against the truth. This wisdom does not descend from above, but is earthly, sensual, demonic. For where envy and self-seeking exist, confusion and every evil thing are there. But the wisdom that is from above is first pure, then peaceable, gentle, willing to yield, full of mercy and good fruits, without partiality and without hypocrisy. Now the fruit of righteousness is sown in peace by those who make peace."

PRAYER

Father God, thank You for Your patience with me. Please forgive me for my selfishness. I've focused on what I don't have instead of praising You for what I do have. Help me to be more grateful. Help me to establish my gifts and talents. I want to see myself the way You see me. I rebuke the spirit of "why her" as it pertains to my sisters and brothers in You. Grant me the spiritual maturity to celebrate those that are blessed around me. Also be with me on my journey to reconcile with anyone I may have sabotaged due to my own insecurities. I empty my shortcomings and hand them to You. I trust You. In Jesus' name, amen.

CLEANSING THOUGHT

There are so many things that hold us back in life. An envious heart is not the anecdote. It's time to get to the root of the behavior that holds us back individually and collectively. Jealousy has no place for us in our growing maturity in Christ. We will use our energy to better ourselves and uplift those around us.

---

1. Can you be honest about a time you've envied someone?
2. In your opinion, what is an anecdote for an envious person?

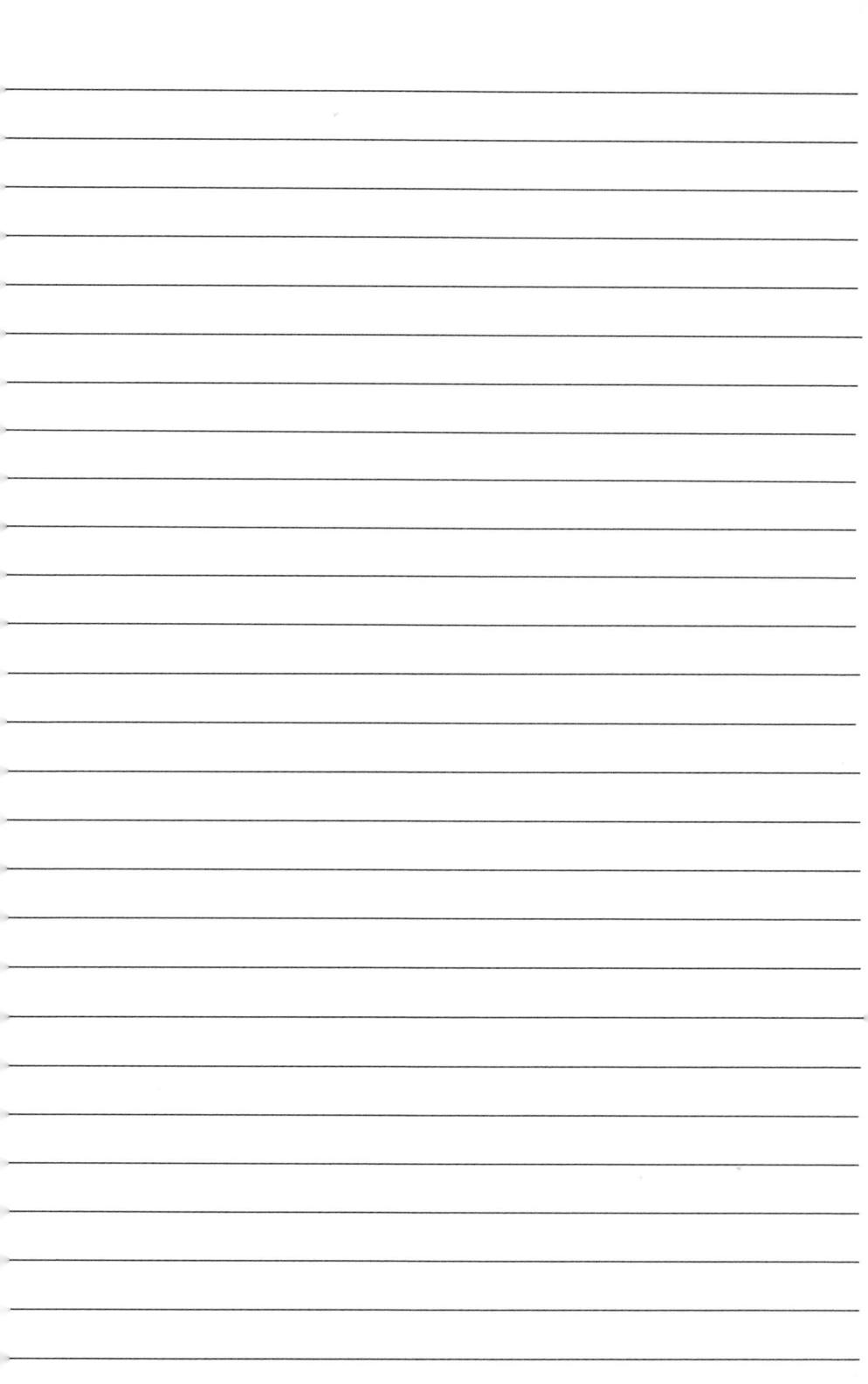

16

SAVED-HOT MESS-UNWATERED

I remember seeing a post on social media from a boy (a grown one) venting about his dating woes. He blamed his misfortune on choosing to date women that were fatherless. He ranted about how daddy's girls were so much easier to deal with and easier to love. He even proclaimed that he wouldn't date a woman if she didn't have a present father in her life. Although there were slivers of truth in his opinion, it didn't compare to the pain he invoked upon every fatherless woman who read his post. How could a man pick apart a demographic of women who had zero control over their father being present or not?

So, I need you to use your best "guess who?" skills because I'm not going to mention her name. But there's this young woman who is a part of a very wealthy and famous family. She's the youngest of her siblings and almost richer than all of them from launching a very successful cosmetic line. A few years ago, a very credible magazine recognized her as a "self-made billionaire". The internet flipped out because everyone felt that she shouldn't have been allowed to tote a self-made title when her success was founded on the success of her wealthy family. Hindsight, the joke is on the trolls because everyone's opinion surely didn't take a dime from her pocket. But I think the discontent that people had, had nothing to do with her billionaire status and had everything to do with the fact that she was taking away the one token that people who are "self-made" have. People who have a lack of support become experts on making something out of nothing and they wear it as a badge of honor. Look at how being a single mother has become a poster child of strength and courage?

We've already touched on the daddy void in an earlier chapter. Fatherlessness is relatable to many people and affects them at all stages of their lives. There are people that lack a family unit all together. Knowing what fatherlessness does to someone, imagine what not having a family at all could do to someone's character and personality. Lacking a foundation of people that have loved you just because you woke up or that got the chance to see you glow up creates a void. They can clearly see others have the support and love and wonder why they don't. A family is supposed to see you at your lowest and still love you the same.

Having a lack of family growing up definitely took a toll on me. It literally strained every relationship I had. Outside of my mother, I didn't know what it was like to be loved unconditionally. Instead, I was loved for what I was good at or what I could produce. From that observation, a terrible habit of people-pleasing was birthed inside of me. Since I didn't get the cousins that would ride or die for me and love me just because...I created it for myself by loving my friends like family. I laid myself out as a sacrifice with such intensity that it spilled over into their families. Before I knew it, I was 18 years old emptying my bank account, cooking, cleaning, doing hair, and even being counsel for entire families just so I could be "one of them." The sad reality is that I wasn't. I was an outsider and the minute I slacked up on my people-pleasing, I realized just how cheap the relationships were.

They never fought for me if I wasn't on my best behavior. They threw me away. I repeated this cycle of sacrificing myself in relationships and trying to be a part of their families over and over again. It wasn't until I was 30 that I realized the toxic cycle I kept riding was birthed from my lack of family. Keep in mind, I'm related to many by blood. The curses are just too deep to have healthy, meaningful relationships. So, I returned to therapy for mental navigation and I turned to God for spiritual navigation. As a grown woman, I remember praying to God that I just wanted to be somebody's baby. I wanted to be valued for existing, not because I could do something for someone.

Like rain in April, God began to water me. He began to reveal my value as His daughter. I learned that I was a part of His royal priesthood and what lovely benefits came with His lineage. Instead of my gifts being used and unappreciated, leaning into God taught me to allow my gifts to make room for me. My tantrums started to transform into gratefulness. I complained about not having enough of a support system to help me with my children, but I realized that my children were my support system. My children were the reset. I could teach them to start with God being their family so they wouldn't have to fall prey to the cycles that plagued me. Just because I made it through something doesn't mean I'd prescribe it for my loved ones.

I don't want any of you to let having a lack of family deplete your value. God has so much to get out of you and it requires confidence. Our confidence is so shallow alone because it is based on so many worldly factors. This is why it's so important to put our confidence in God. His confidence has no boundaries and is omnipotent just like Him. He can give you all the water you need to grow. So don't feel depleted the next time you see someone elevated based on the family they have. You too have the ultimate connection. He can shine a light on you wherever you are.

PSALM 68:3-6 NKJV

"But let the righteous be glad; Let them rejoice before God; Yes, let them rejoice exceedingly. Sing to God, sing praises to His name; Extol Him who rides on the clouds, By His name YAH, And rejoice before Him. A father of the fatherless, a defender of widows, Is God in His holy habitation. God sets the solitary in families; He brings out those who are bound into prosperity."

PRAYER

Father God, I'm coming to You as Your child. I love You so much and thank You for keeping me thus far. Please forgive me for my shortcomings. I need You. The physical family that You placed me in has let me down. I put expectations on them and they came up short. I now want to practice putting expectations on You. I expect You to protect me, defend me, understand and love me just like Your word says. Water me, God, in every unwatered part of my life so the premature areas of my mind, body, and spirit can grow. I love You and I trust You. In Jesus' name, amen.

CLEANSING THOUGHT

Lots of us are walking around as children in adult bodies. We blame our childhood voids for our stumbling blocks. As valid as our problems are, they are not bigger than God. He created us to be a part of His wonder and grace and to live out our purpose, confidently. We have power through our Father in heaven. So receive the rain! There's a great blooming ahead and you're a part of it.

1. Considering the level of support or lack of you received during your upbringing, how were you supported? In what ways were you not supported?
2. What are ways you can invite God to water you?

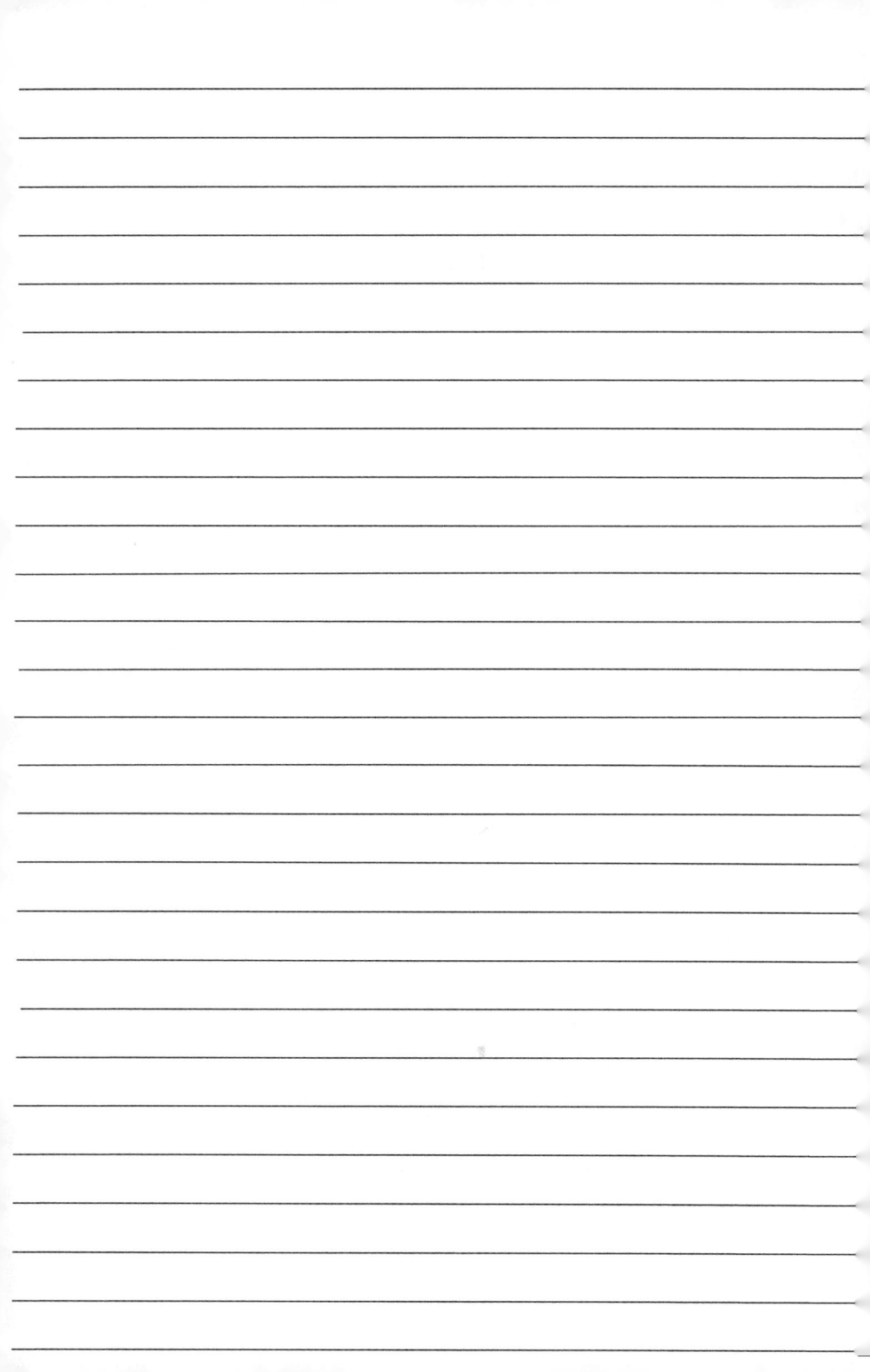

17

GIFTS-SAVED HOT MESS-RECYCLING

Recycling is the process of collecting and processing materials that would otherwise be thrown away as trash and turning them into new products.[1] As a society we have perfected the practice of looking at trash or something unwanted and finding a way to repurpose it. I'm grateful for this practice. It has halted forecasted global destruction and made resources available to the human race. It's now second nature to look at an empty soda can or even a grocery bag and see it as recyclable. However, for some reason we don't look at our own lives in the same light.

As humans who have an expected physical death, one would think that we would consistently recycle our gifts and life experiences in order to repurpose them for our future. All too often the opposite happens. If our life experiences are less than perfect or sometimes shameful, we have the urge to bury that part of us. We associate the fall with failure. Believe me, I get it. When we make mistakes or find ourselves in an unfavorable situation, it can be humiliating and embarrassing. If you have the strength to make it through whatever it is you experience, the last

---

[1] Recycling basics. (2020, November 12). Retrieved April, 2021, from https://www.epa.gov/recycle/recycling-basics

thing you want to do is examine the situation for fear of reliving it. But I have this hunch...maybe God gives us the gift of memory and recollection in order to learn from our mistakes and be a better version of ourselves afterwards. A new, shiny diamond ring wrapped in a fine jeweler's box is a wonderful gift to receive from someone. It's thoughtful and has value. Imagine that same ring being worn by a woman for 2 generations. Imagine this woman working with that ring on, following her dreams with that ring on, raising her children, defying odds, and overcoming and then regifting it to her granddaughter. The ring now has more value because it has a story and a purpose. That is the way God wants us to view our lives. Our lives are worth living because they give us a blueprint of how we were able to live through it. Someone else watching may need your blueprint to keep going.

I have been through so much in life but one particular situation that I had a hard time finding peace with was the failure of my marriage. When I separated from my husband and realized that the vows I made to God were no longer honored, I was so disappointed in myself. I tried everything virtually possible to save my marriage. I prayed fervently, I cried, I sought therapy, I sought counsel from other married couples, I changed my hair, I changed my routine, I cooked more, I tried to kiss up to his family, and I had enough sex to run a brothel. I even forgave the most unforgivable acts and it still wasn't enough. When it was time to redefine or recycle myself, I realized something. The experience that caused me to look at myself as a failure was really a gift. The gumption that it took to stick to something that wasn't serving me was the same gumption I needed to elevate myself. It didn't save my marriage, but it saved me as I navigated my divorce. God allowed me to be recycled instead of thrown away. I now possess a wisdom and strength that I wouldn't have unless I experienced that type of heartache and disappointment. The greatest gift is my testimony. It's not to bring me glory or paint me as a victor but to show someone else how they can overcome a trash situation and be renewed. Don't get me wrong, the recycling process is rough. It requires crushing, breaking, a lot of fire, and meltdowns. However, it turns into something new, something useful, something worthy.

JOHN 6:12 NKJV

"So when they were filled, He said to His disciples, 'Gather up the fragments that remain, so that nothing is lost.' Therefore they gathered them up, and filled twelve baskets with the fragments of the five barley loaves which were left over by those who had eaten."

PRAYER

God of yesterday, today, and forever, thank You for Your provision. Thank You for hindsight, as painful as it is. In the past, I resented You for allowing me to go through trashy seasons in my life. Please forgive me for not understanding Your transformative power. I no longer wish to view myself as trash but wish to be recycled for Your good. Use me in the most resourceful way. Create in me a clean heart. In Jesus' name, amen.

CLEANSING THOUGHT

Do not take for granted the wins tucked into hurtful experiences. Recycle that heartache and pain and realize the strength that you needed to maneuver the situations necessary for you to gain wisdom. Each lesson you learn is adding value to your life and those around you. Congratulations in advance because you are a gift; recycled and new at the same time.

---

1. List some of your gifts.
2. Did you discover your gifts on purpose or by circumstances? Give examples.

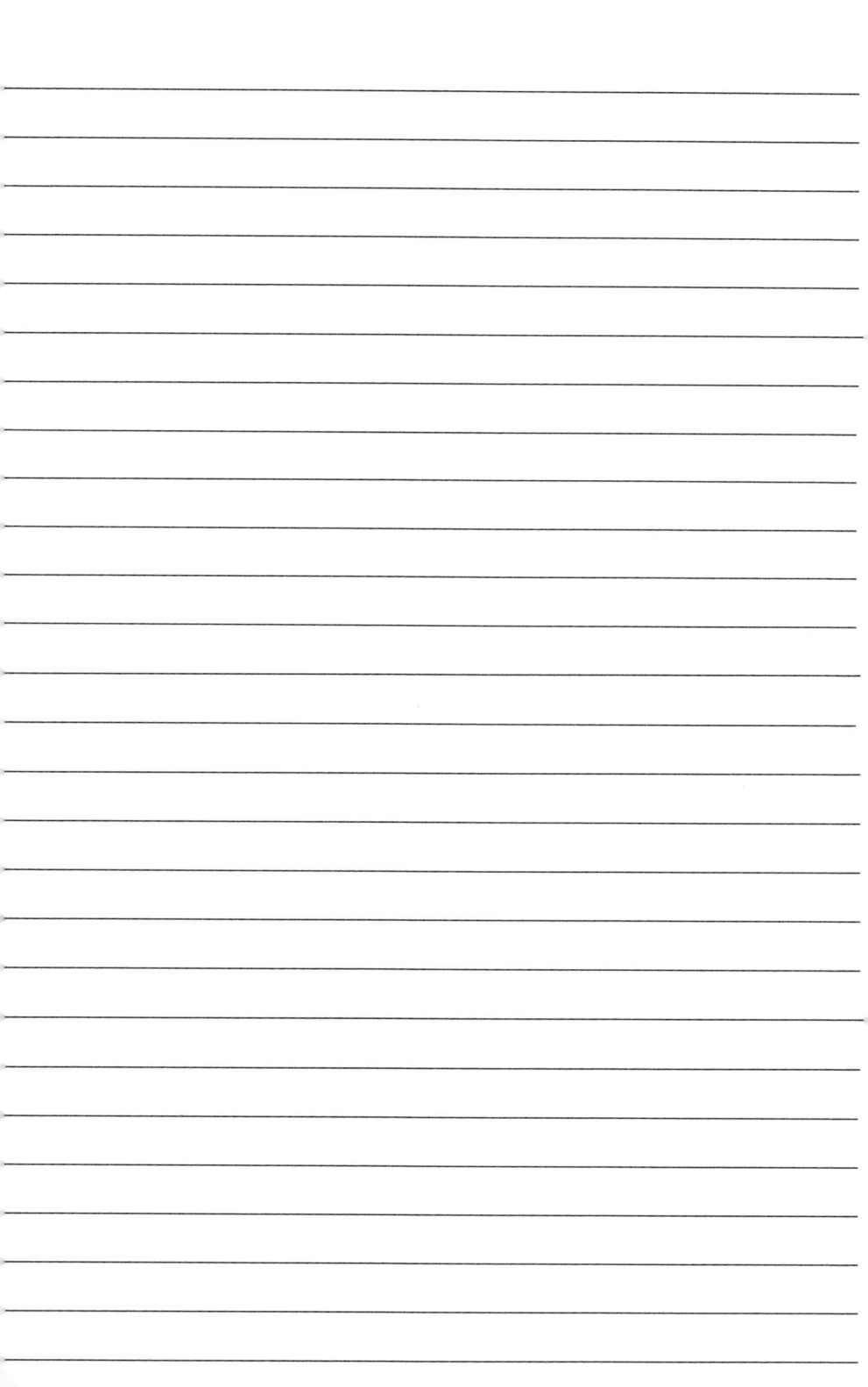

18

SAVED · HOT MESS · OVER EASY ·

No one was more intrigued than me to learn about anti-slut shaming initiatives. The walks, podcasts, and protests that began to emerge in 2016 were all well overdue. Girls and women should have agency over their own bodies and minds regarding their own sexuality. The awareness of that meant the world to a woman like me. When I say, "a woman like me," I'm referring to women that have sex before marriage. I'm referring to women that wear dresses above their knees, who might also like to wear red lipstick. I'm referring to women that may have had more than one boyfriend in their lifetime. Men are often raised to sow their wild oats. Even in the church, "boys be boys". We lightheartedly joke about how boys begin to take long showers as teens or some other self-exploration jokes when it comes to boys. That's not the case for girls. Girls are shamed for their body development, especially in the black community. If a girl shakes her hips too hard she is labeled as "fast" and monitored closely to try to halt sexual behavior. There is even a terrible notion that if a girl's hips widen, a sign of puberty, that she is likely having sex. Imagine being a terrified 10-year-old whose idea of action is the cartoon dogs kissing from "Lady and the Tramp" and people are chastising you.

"Girl, we gotta watch you!"

"Them hips spreading, you betta not be having sex."

"You can't wear what they have on, they're skinny and you're not."

And if you can't imagine it getting any worse, imagine being molested and overcoming it, yet being treated as if your developed body was the reason it happened to you. It's such a sad reality for a lot of us, but that's not what God made us for. Everything that God made was good. Now, I'm not saying God gives His blessings for us to throw our bodies at anything with legs. What I am saying is that a lot of times we focus on shame and we should focus on love. Love covers a multitude of sins. I often punish myself for ways that I mentally maneuver topics like intimacy and sexuality. I enjoy physical touch and pleasure more than I'd like to admit. Only God knows how I became this way, but that's enough reason to not beat myself up about my shortcomings. My love for God should exceed my shame. I've made many mistakes with my body. I will probably make many more. I'm not easy because I don't fit into societal norms regarding Christian women. When I repent, God keeps no record of my sin. I can't let anyone else condemn me into shame.

JOHN 8:2-12 NKJV

"Now early in the morning He came again into the temple, and all the people came to Him; and He sat down and taught them. Then the scribes and Pharisees brought to Him a woman caught in adultery. And when they had set her in the midst, they said to Him, "Teacher, this woman was caught in adultery, in the very act. Now Moses, in the law, commanded us that such should be stoned. But what do You say?"

This they said, testing Him, that they might have something of which to accuse Him. But Jesus stooped down and wrote on the ground with His finger, as though He did not hear. So when they continued asking Him, He raised Himself up and said to them, "He who is without sin among you, let him throw a stone at her first." And again He stooped down and wrote on the ground. Then those who heard it, being convicted by their conscience, went out one by one, beginning with the oldest even to the last. And Jesus was left alone, and the woman standing in the midst. When Jesus had raised Himself up and saw no one but the woman, He said to her, "Woman, where are those accusers of yours? Has no one condemned you?" She said, "No one, Lord." And Jesus said to her, "Neither do I condemn you; go and sin no more." Then Jesus spoke to them again, saying, "I am the light of the world. He who follows Me shall not walk in darkness, but have the light of life."

PRAYER

Father God, I love You so much for loving me the way I am. You made no mistakes in creating me and allowing me to experience life in a way that strengthens Your purpose for me. Forgive me for my sins. I've fallen short and fallen away. There are people that try to disqualify me from Your kingdom and that have judged me from their pedestals. Deliver me from overly-sanctified and equally guilty Christians that misrepresent You. Let nothing come between You and me. In Jesus' name, amen.

CLEANSING THOUGHT

We were born into sin of all sorts. For some reason, as a culture we more harshly condemn sins of our bodies. We must start viewing ourselves as God sees us. We should move closer to God when we make mistakes or need to find our way. A lot of times we are disqualified by people and think it's by God. We must not forget why Jesus died for us. He died so we would not live in shame. Be faultless and shameless before His eyes just as He created you to be.

---

1.   Has promiscuity ever been a challenge for you? Explain.
2.   How do you think God feels about promiscuity?

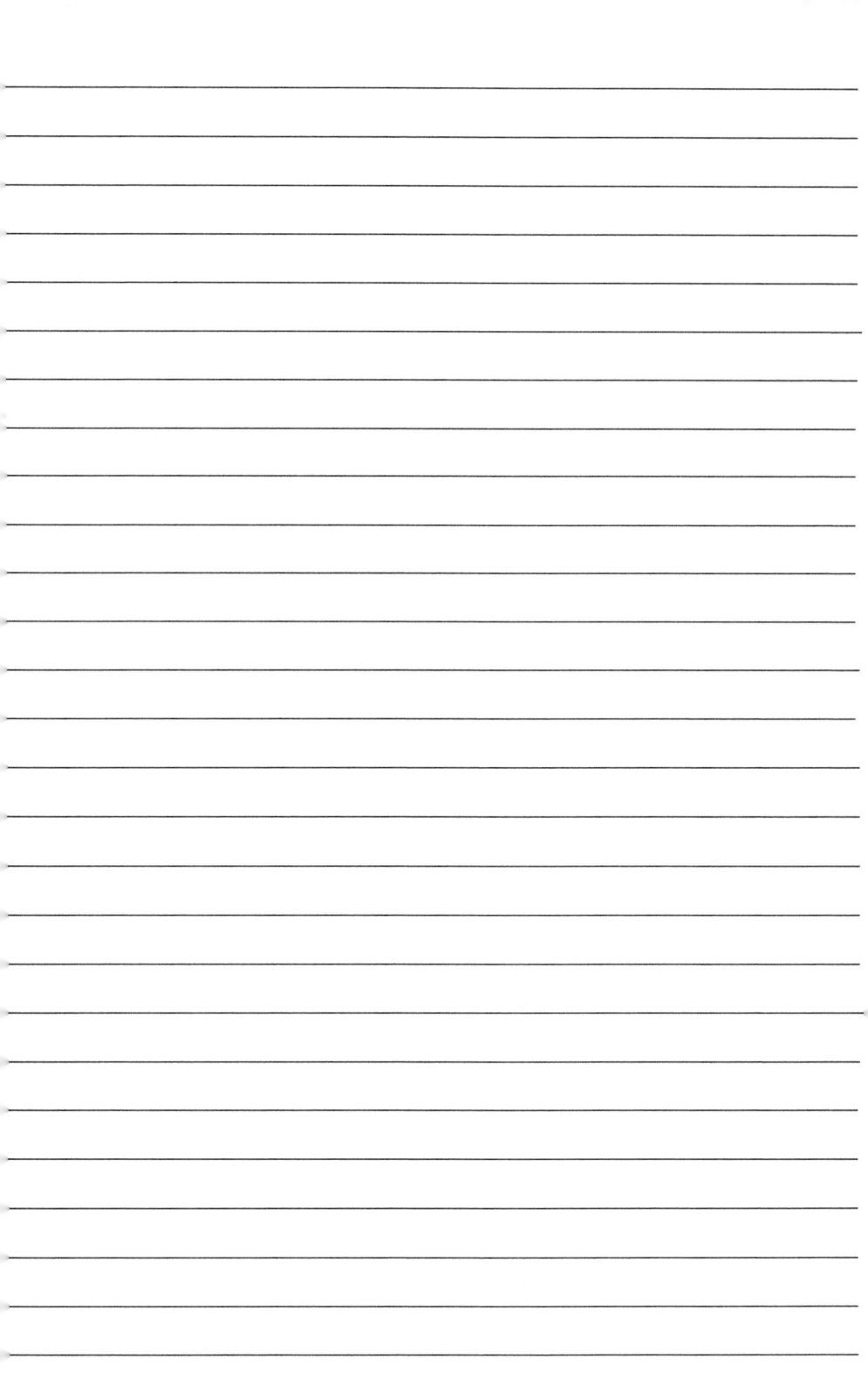

19

In a world where every cute couple on social media is relationship goals and extravagant proposals are a bigger milestone than diplomas, everybody who's anybody wants a relationship. It's especially romanticized for women. Our worth is magically doubled when we have a man. Women appear more important, more beautiful, more successful, and even envied for having a man on their side. Even if the man isn't the best looking, or smart, or successful...the saying goes, "It's better to have half of a man than none at all." This narrative is indoctrinated into us culturally from our first Disney movie viewing experience.

Princess Jasmine had it all but needed Aladdin to have "a whole new world." Ariel was willing to risk her inheritance to be a part of Eric's. Even Princess Tiana had to get it out the mud with Prince Naveen before she finally achieved her dreams. Life appears to be good but it's great if you have a man. So I, along with every adolescent, helpless romantic, fell prey to the same ideology as an adult. My life was good but it would only be great after a man loved me and claimed me as his own. I posted my feelings on social media about wanting to find a king and, looking back, I actually gave the blueprint to my heart away. I shared memes that agreed with my sentiments and longed for date nights and cuddle sessions.

"When I get married..." posts could have had their own archives as much as I was obsessed with being wanted. Men began to bite on the vibes I sent. As they casually pursued me, I waited for someone to get on with it. I wanted a man to "put the pressure on me" and remove me from singledom. The more desperate I was, the less walls I had up, and the more liberal I became about what I wanted and deserved. I went from having a standard of being provided for to thinking that joblessness and lack of motivation wasn't so bad. Nobody's perfect, right? As long as I had a man.

So, I finally got the man that I wanted so bad. In the beginning, he pursued me, but by our first disagreement, the roles switched. He showed me how unready he was to build anything with me and I began the pursuit of him. I don't know why we think we can change the trajectory of a broken man with love. That's just like trying to build a house with bricks made of water.

There's more to be said about the insecurity that exists to even fall into this type of entanglement but let's focus on the pursuit for now. God did not design us to chase after a man, especially just to say we have one. He actually designed us to accentuate and be loved by a man who finds us. I know this notion might seem antiquated and old school but in all honesty, it works. The successful, long-term relationships that I admire subscribe to this sentiment. God designed, described, and destined women in such a beautiful and magnificent way. Many times we let popular culture steer us away from our destiny. Furthermore, it takes 2 whole humans to successfully have a relationship. A lot of us need to address the issues in our own world before we join someone else's. We have to put all of that thirst for love into a thirst for bettering ourselves. The right mate will be drawn to us and make us wonder why we thought we could have done a better job in the first place.

PROVERBS 18:22 ESV

"He who finds a wife finds a good thing, And obtains favor from the LORD."

PRAYER

Heavenly Father, thank You for loving me so I can love others. Please forgive me for discrediting love. I've been hurt and betrayed where love should've been. I need a restructuring of my heart. I declare that I will attract a healthy man that loves You fervently and that will love me in a healthy and beneficial way. I'm asking for patience and wisdom along the way. In Jesus' name, amen.

CLEANSING THOUGHT

Women are strong. It comes quite natural to us. Maybe that's why God gave such simple instructions regarding our courting process. Once we get in a relationship, we do a lot of work to keep it functioning and afloat. It's time for these men to put in the work to keep us. We also can't be misguided by worldly appetizers and miss the feast He has for us.

---

1.   What are your expectations when dating or considering a mate? Spiritually? Physically? Emotionally?

2.   How does your self-value measure up to what you prefer in a mate?

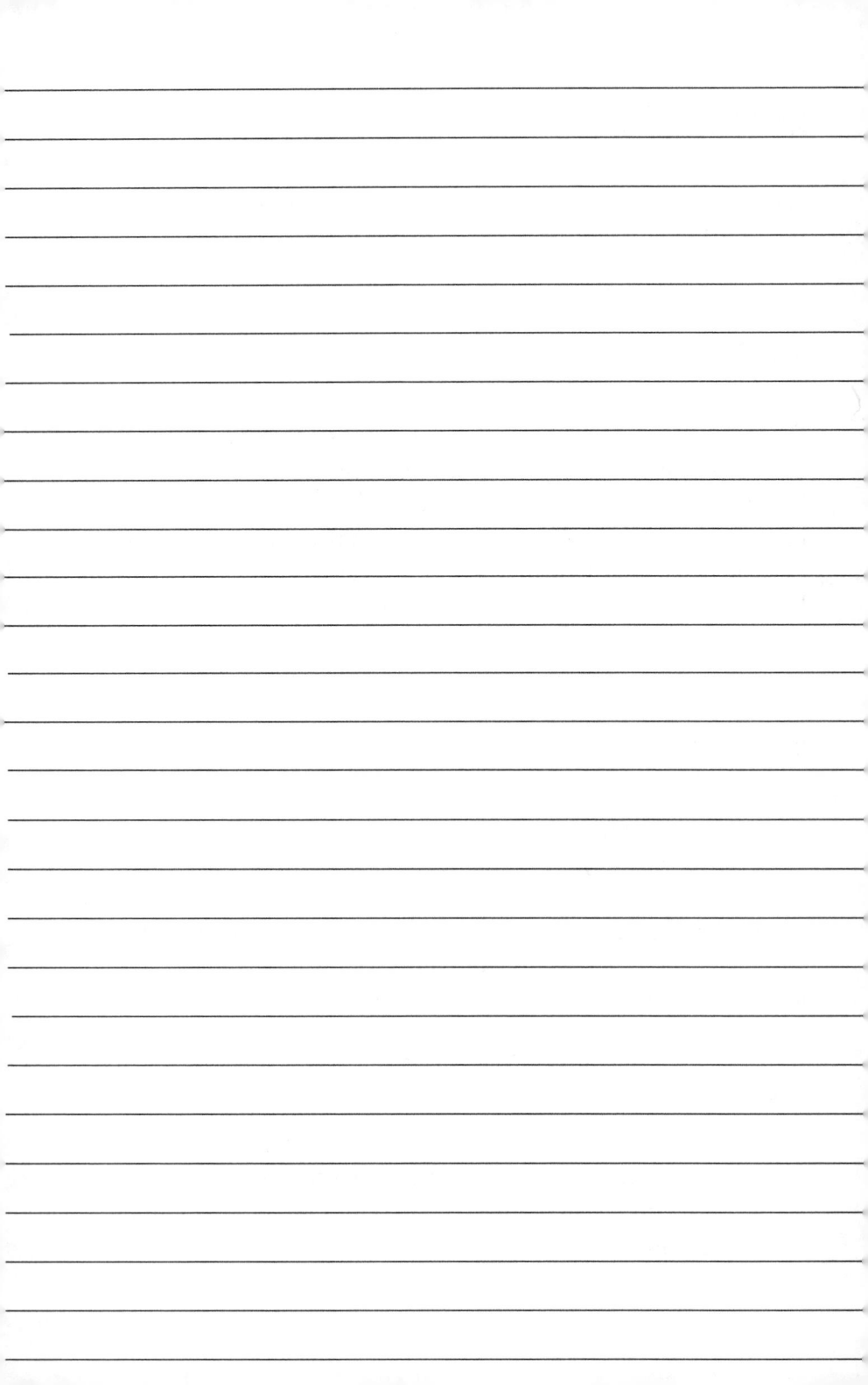

BROKEN -SAVED HOT MESS- BARREN -BUT NOT

20

As the proud founder of the "Saved Hot Mess" community, I realized when writing this book how large the umbrella of those who can relate to any message in this book would be. I had to consider what I would touch on that directly affected me. I also had to consider what subjects affected my loved ones and other women (and men) in my demographic. One sensitive subject that has caused a lot of pain and confusion for a lot of women in my life has been infertility. The mere mention of it makes my stomach drop and takes my breath away. I have to admit, I have never struggled with it personally, but speaking on it aligned with the word of God might help bring more awareness to the topic, spiritually and emotionally. As I searched for the title of this chapter I asked friends, co-workers, and even clients if they had ever struggled or knew someone that did so I could be accurate about the information that I would share. I was so overwhelmed by the response.

There were women who shared their experience with pain so thick it could be cut with a knife. Then there were women who couldn't hold back the tears. The most common response was feeling as if they weren't whole due to infertility. Any advice I had to offer seemed void of depth. These women shared a fate that seemed so unfair in our indulgent world. Social media is flooded with messy situationships that flaunt their designer babies for vain consumption. Some women are out here using abortion as birth control. And then you have these faithful women, many of whom are married and very deserving of a child, who are struggling. Month after month, year after year, these women are let down and reminded of what they perceive as being incomplete. What devotional content can uplift a woman or couple navigating this complex and painful situation?

I'll tell you what I won't do. I won't sit here and say how God blessed an elderly woman and man with a baby so just wait on the Lord. Nor will I throw a pity party. I will say marvel at the sight of strength that is both rare and particularly divine. To every woman struggling with infertility, know that although your womb has let you down countless times by only birthing disappointment and doubt, you are not broken. You are painfully beautiful and your will to keep going and love the way you do is so inspiring. When I talk with women who have battled with infertility, they usually have the biggest, most giving hearts. Children gravitate towards them and they display agape love in a pure, precious way. If I could personify God's love, a love that is seamless and flowing even with deterrents in the way, it flows from a woman who is barren but not broken.

If it's not too selfish, I ask that if you are battling with this, please don't do it alone. I know you might have shame and confusion. You might be angry. That's understandable, but people like me want to understand and support you. We want to love on you throughout your journey. Your strength is unmatched and I thank God in advance for your individual and collective testimonies. It's my belief that those of you that bear this load are the spiritual daughters of Job. The strength and endurance you model is an exquisite example for many of us to emulate.

JOB 42:12-16

"Now the LORD blessed the latter days of Job more than his beginning; for he had fourteen thousand sheep, six thousand camels, one thousand yoke of oxen, and one thousand female donkeys. He also had seven sons and three daughters. And he called the name of the first Jemimah, the name of the second Keziah, and the name of the third Keren-Happuch. In all the land were found no women so beautiful as the daughters of Job; and their father gave them an inheritance among their brothers. After this Job lived one hundred and forty years, and saw his children and grandchildren for four generations."

PRAYER

Dearest God, thank You for life, strength, and the pursuit of happiness. I honor Your grace and love for me. Forgive me for my unbelief. It's hard to serve You so earnestly and not get what I have prayed for. It's hard to see others have what I believe that I deserve. I'm human and limited in what I can see and what I can do. This is why I need You, God. I need Your wisdom and strength to endure. I need Your love to overcome the pain that I've experienced. I need a reminder that I am connected to You and of a royal priesthood. I rebuke the hardening of my heart and embrace all that You have and will have for me. In Jesus' name, amen.

---

1.   Why do you think society has deemed motherhood a necessity for womanhood?
2.   Outside of motherhood...what makes you valuable?

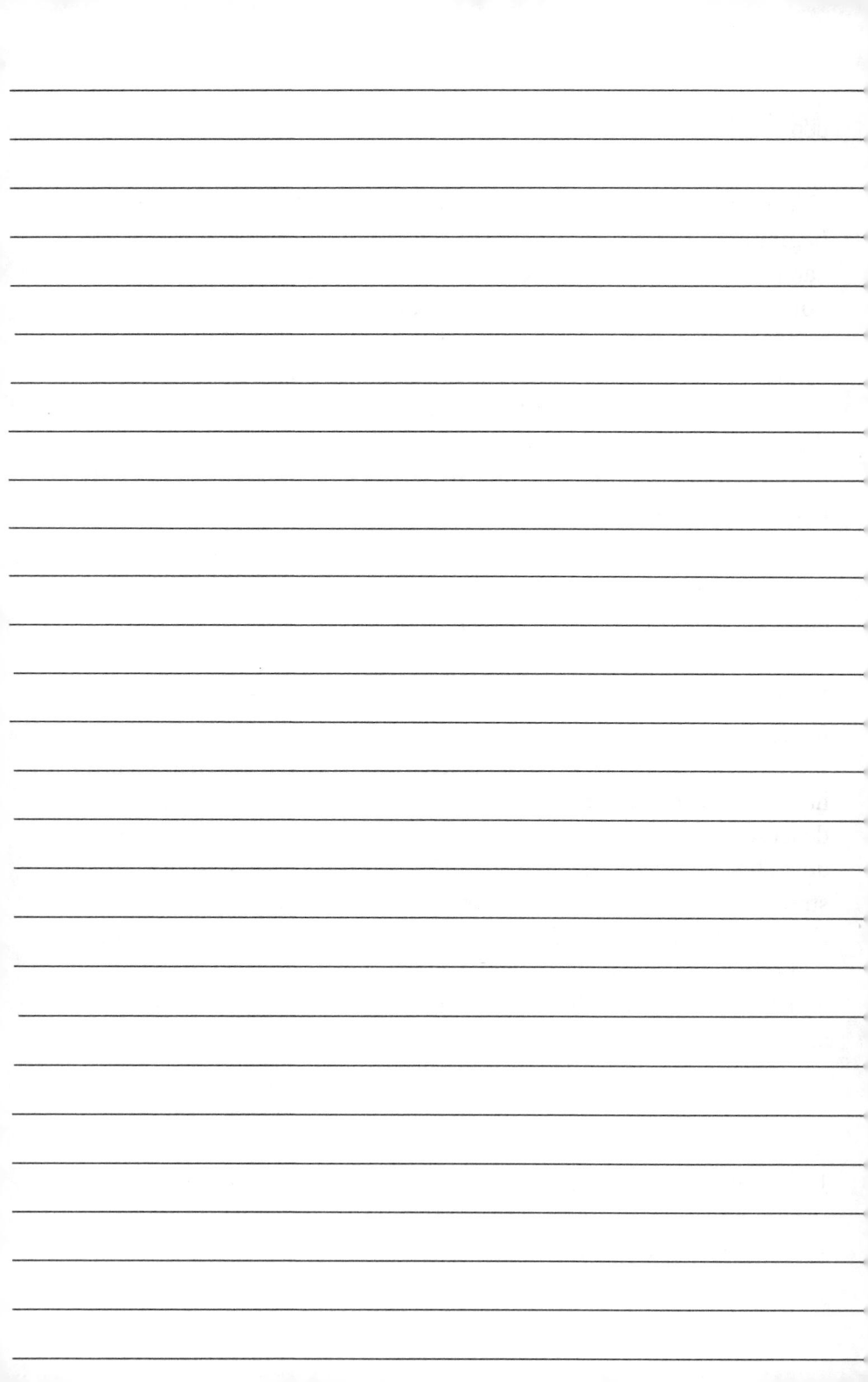

All of the greatest stories have heroes and villains. Simba and Mufasa. Ariel and Ursula. David and Goliath and so forth. It's evident that in order for the hero to do their best hero work they need a menace to make their job much harder. The balance of the two makes the victory much sweeter. I can't tell you how many times I've yelled at a tv screen to try to warn the hero of what the enemy was doing to plot the hero's demise. I'm okay with knowing that the enemy is there but I also feel like more can be done to protect the hero from letting the enemy even think they have a chance of winning.

We all have a common enemy. He's notorious by now and even though Jesus did his thang on the cross for us, the enemy is still mad and goes out of his way to come against our souls. Where we go wrong is assuming that the enemy will be blatant with horns, a pitch fork, and a name tag. A lot of times the enemy comes where he's invited and appears in the most enticing way. Instead of guarding ourselves, we enable him. I'll give you a hypothetical example.

I have a friend who has an issue with drinking heavily. Their drinking has led to property being damaged, people's lives being at risk, and trust being broken. Said friend does the work necessary to get closer to healing and sobriety and positions themselves to live a healthier lifestyle. What sense does it make for them to gather at a bar? The enemy, in the form of alcoholism, will be waiting for them at the door.

We also enable the enemy with our mouths. There is power in the tongue; life or death power. We are so quick to speak boldly about our vices. Don't get me wrong. Transparency and testimony are lit, but openly admitting our weaknesses to the wrong people can definitely enable and entice the enemy. I remember I thought it was so cool to hear popular music talk about having trust issues. I started to brag about my own. I remember even putting it into an "about me" section on social media. It invited people that meant me no good to get me to trust them. Just like the snake in the garden, they broke my trust and betrayed me. I should have proclaimed that I was building trust or even spoke that I trusted God. Instead, I enabled the enemy and made myself an easy target. The enemy is evil, but not stupid. We often forget that he was once an angel and for that reason, he is jealous of our grace. This is why we should always pray for God to protect us and for angels to encamp around us as we come and go. For every angel there's a dark spirit waiting to block your light at all times. There's no way to escape this but don't put a target on your back by enabling your enemies with the ammo to take you out.

MATHEW 10:16-22 ESV

"Behold, I am sending you out as sheep in the midst of wolves, so be wise as serpents and innocent as doves. Beware of men, for they will deliver you over to courts and flog you in their synagogues, and you will be dragged before governors and kings for my sake, to bear witness before them and the Gentiles. When they deliver you over, do not be anxious how you are to speak or what you are to say, for what you are to say will be given to you in that hour. For it is not you who speak, but the Spirit of your Father speaking through you. Brother will deliver brother over to death, and the father his child, and children will rise against parents and have them put to death, and you will be hated by all for my name's sake. But the one who endures to the end will be saved."

PRAYER

Father God, my protector, I come to You, thanking You so much for Your wisdom. I've looked over my life and take responsibility for putting myself in situations that make me vulnerable to the enemy. I should only be vulnerable to You. Please forgive me. Help me to discern my tongue and my actions as to no longer enable the enemy. He has no power here. In Jesus' name, amen.

CLEANSING THOUGHT

Yes, we were born into sin. These women are bad and these men are fine. God made the fruit that makes the wine and the seed that makes sativa...but He also gave us wisdom and free will. We all know our vices and should never enable them. All they eventually know how to do is get us into situations that we want to avoid. Don't give the enemy the knife to stab you in the back.

1. What is the best posture to have when encountering an enemy?
2. Have you identified the purpose of the enemy attempting to derail your life?

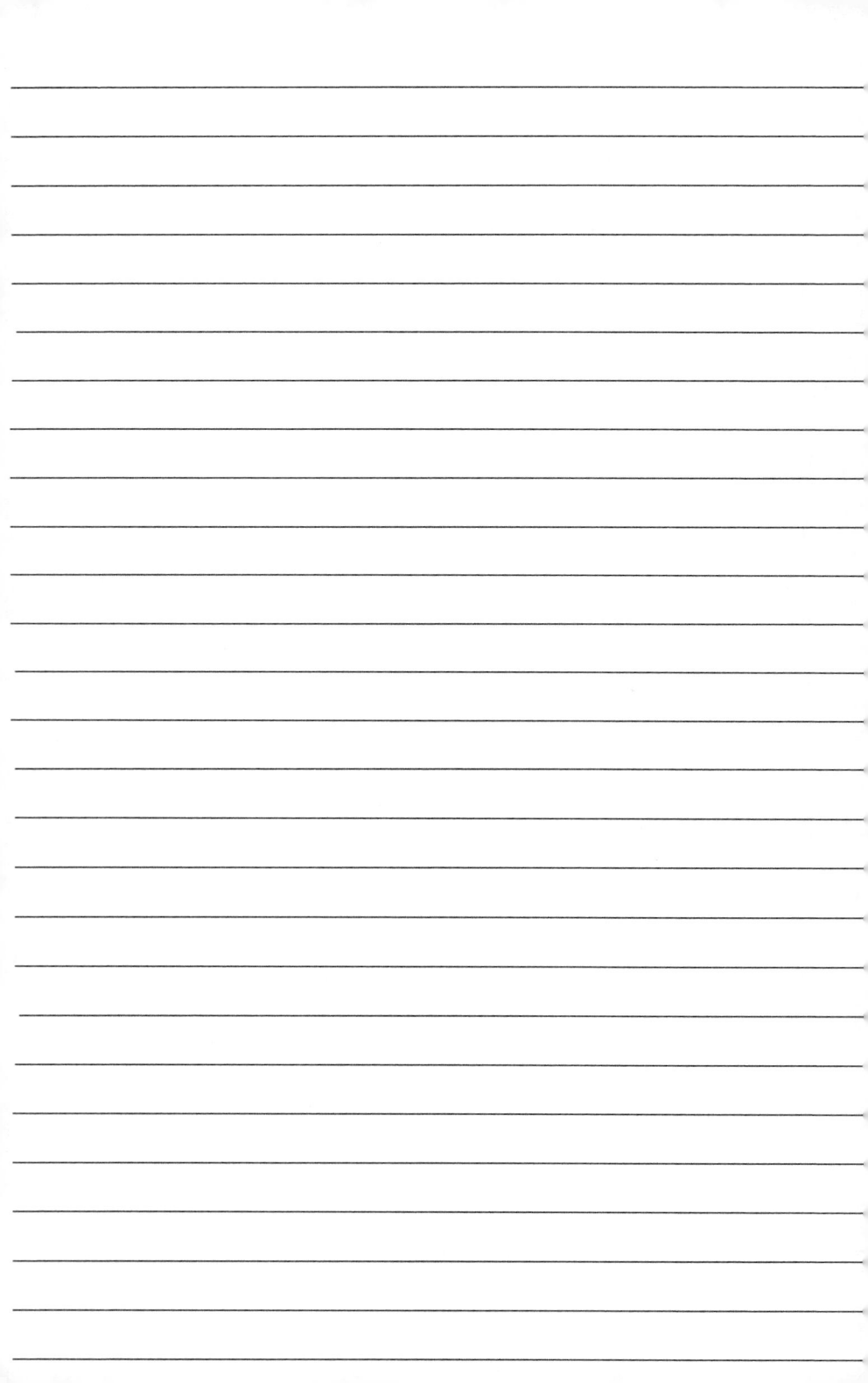

22

CAPTOR -SAVED HOT MESS - MY KINKS AND THEIR

T his is the chapter that will either get me into heaven for writing it, or get me shunned by the church for bringing it up. Imagine a princess being locked away in a cage with a beast. The princess wants nothing more in life than to be set free but the beast is the only one with the key to let her out. That's the best way to describe my sexuality.

Sexual pleasure is a coping mechanism for me. When I'm stressed, overwhelmed, overworked, tired, or just blah, I can always count on "the big O" to mellow me out. It's readily available (I can have it alone or with someone else) and it's natural and reliable. The reason it's a beast is because of how I became this way. My innocence was disturbed as a child and that caused me to explore it early on. When I should've connected to other things that felt good, the kink of sexual stimulation got to me first. I spent years chasing, exploring, and finding out ways to satisfy my kinks. Sometimes it was socially acceptable and sometimes it was dangerous.

Sparing the details so this won't come off as erotica, I have created an idolatrous relationship with sex. I would often ask myself why would God create a feeling that was so amazing and then limit our ability to access it? The answer is in denying our flesh. Our flesh is beautiful indeed. We were made in His image and He put every sensation, nerve, and hormone in perfect place. Our bodies are made to experience a high without any extra stimulant or drug. But we are not just flesh. We also have a soul. Our soul has a destination based on the handling of our flesh. I believe it's God's desire for us to live a balanced life where our mind, flesh, and soul give honor to Him. Over indulging our flesh leaves no room for our soul to flourish. I figured that out from trial and error.

Did the beast ever give the princess the key? The answer is no. The beast never will. The beast actually dangles the key and comes in the form of attractive men and women, scenic parties, and fantasies of temporary satisfaction. So, I decided to take my kinks to God in prayer. It was hard to talk to God about sex and being horny. My shame and fault kept me from it for a long time, but He wants us to be blameless before Him. We have to stop acting shameful to a God that sees everything and knows our thoughts. There's so much freedom in knowing our kinks and asking God to iron them out. I'm not saying temptation won't come, but the purpose of this devotional is to get us closer to the cross. Progress is better than stagnation.

1 CORINTHIANS 10: 23-24 NKJV

"All things are lawful for me, but not all things are helpful; all things are lawful for me, but not all things edify. Let no one seek his own, but each one the other's well-being. Eat whatever is sold in the meat market, asking no questions for conscience' sake; for "the earth is the LORD's, and all its fullness."

PRAYER

Oh Holy Father, hear my prayer. Thank You for reflection. You created desire, love, comfort, and sex. The world perverted it and made it for mindless consumption. I've fallen into patterns of sexual immorality. It has caused me guilt and shame. I know that You want me to be faultless before You. Help me fight my urge to live in my flesh. I want to honor you in all my ways. Help me replace my desire for physical thrills with a desire to be closer to You. I love You with all of my heart. In Jesus' name, amen.

CLEANSING THOUGHT

We are more than our kinks. We are more than our flesh. Our whole being has a purpose which is why we should enrich our minds with knowledge, elevate our souls with prayer, and fulfill our bodies with health. We should do it to give God the glory. That practice alone will make little room for kinks and entanglements.

1. Have you ever felt guilty about your sexuality? How did that come about?
2. What has church taught you about sex? Were your questions about this topic answered?

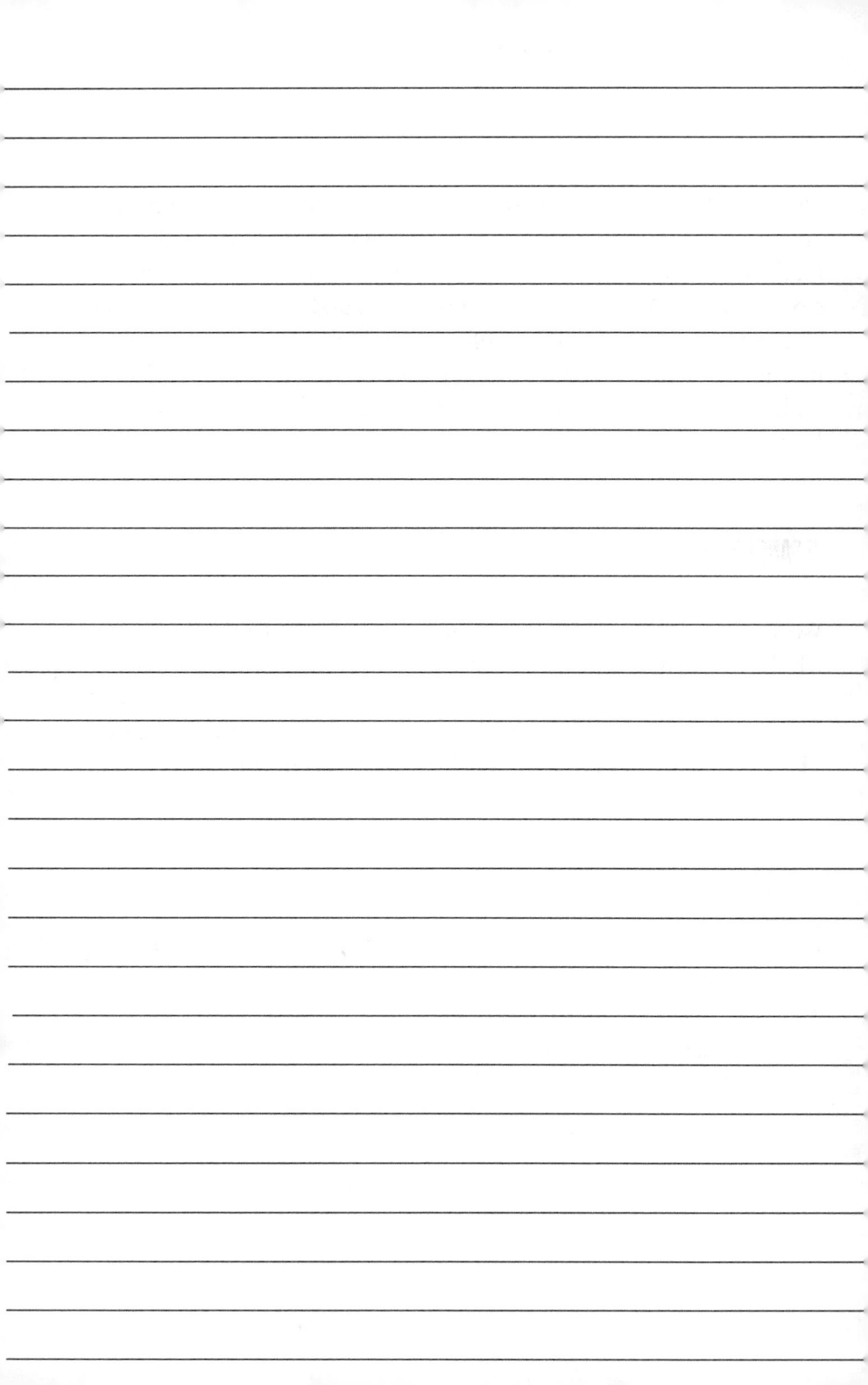

BUILDING -SAVED HOT MESS -FAITH

23

If faith was a standing, tangible building and pieces of our lives were the bricks that built it, what would the foundation consist of? Would it be our reputation? Would it be wealth? How about people? Here's a clear way to find out. What's important to you? What's the first thing you think of doing when you arise? When we ask God to search us, we are never ready for the way He will reveal things in us. That's how I felt writing this chapter.

Biblically, our faith should rest in the fact that God is all powerful and that He has agape love for us. However, I can't help but think about everything else when I'm in a tight spot. A lot of times when I'm going through something I'm worried about what others will think of me. I worry about how I can financially afford for a problem to go away. I worry about how my mistake will affect others and go on a spiritual self-imploding journey. It's hella toxic. In those instances, my faith house would surely fall. Imagine if I inserted faith as soon as problems arose. My bills are due...faith. He doesn't want me anymore...faith. My kids won't listen...faith. She stole my idea...faith. They lied on me...faith. Another negative pregnancy test...faith. Anything that you can think of...faith. As we are tested, our faith either grows or shrinks. The variable is whether we activate it boldly or not.

Some of us misheard preachers when they told us about Jesus telling the disciples to have faith the size of a mustard seed. He didn't say that as a stand alone statement. He was giving them a lesson after they exhibited unbelief. We can't claim unbelief. We have all seen God work miracles on our behalf. I dare you to speak your most recent miracle out loud. Really speak it. And see how tangible our faith can be. Yes, faith of a mustard seed is beautiful and honorable, but some of us can build ours up past that. It's our duty to do so. Our faith will encourage others.

Faith is the winning shot. It's our secret weapon against all the things that plague us. We have to be intentional about it. We have to build our faith like we're building our bodies for hot girl summers.

ISAIAH 43:2 WEB

"When you pass through the waters, I will be with you; And through the rivers, they shall not overflow you. When you walk through the fire, you shall not be burned, Nor shall the flame scorch you. For I am the LORD your God, The Holy One of Israel, your Savior; I gave Egypt for your ransom, Ethiopia and Seba in your place. Since you were precious in My sight, You have been honored, And I have loved you; Therefore I will give men for you, And people for your life. Fear not, for I am with you; I will bring your descendants from the east, And gather you from the west;"

PRAYER

Faithful God,

Thank You for being an ever present figure in my life. I'm sorry for my transgressions, please forgive me. I've been let down and I've blamed You. It has affected my faith in You. Help me remember the times Your power has rescued me. Hold my hand as I build my faith to better navigate this world. In Jesus' name, amen.

CLEANSING THOUGHT

God is not a one trick pony. He is an all powerful, all knowing force with the ability to change everything with the blink of an eye. We don't have to suffer spiritually when we go through tough situations. We can take the load from our own shoulders and put it on Him. After making a practice of it, we will no longer wonder if God will come but we'll expect Him to.

1.   In your own words define "faith".
2.   What are some ways you can strengthen your faith?

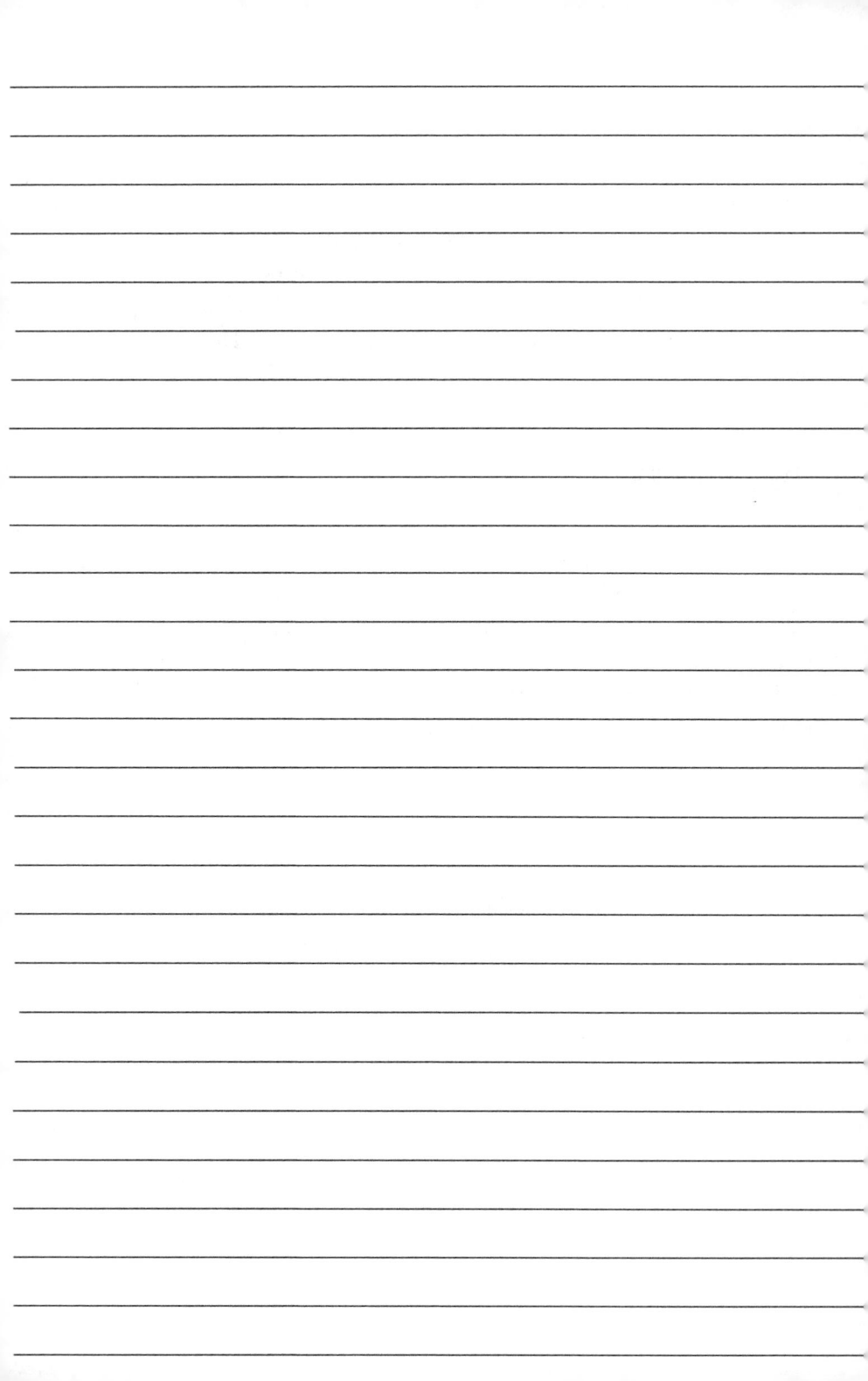

24

ore hips, swollen ankles, working long hours, letdowns, heartbreaks, butt kissing, sacrifices, lack of sleep, saying yes when I wanted to say no and saying no when I wanted to say yes...sounds appealing huh? Although unglamorous, this is sometimes motherhood. This is the bittersweet part that's never talked about. God forbid a mother be anything less than perfect, she'd be labeled as ungrateful, unfit, or even unforgivable. Society is hard on mothers. We are expected to always deliver and to do it gracefully. But just to keep it all the way a hundred, it's downright tiring sometimes. The sacrifice is worth the love I have for my children but I constantly ask myself who am I running myself ragged for?

There have been many times that I've thrown over the top parties for my children but it seemed more like my party instead. Is it possible that we over exert ourselves for our own self-righteousness? Or are we shallow enough to believe we can buy our children's love? I know that I do not benefit from the superwoman-ing that I do. It takes away from me and breaks me down. Sometimes, a part of me wants to undo some of the wrongs I experienced as a child. I remember my pastor, Dr. Robert Charles Scott saying, "Parents are too busy giving their children what they never had but failed to give them what they did have...respect, patience, courtesy, manners, etc" Whew! That hit different for me as a young parent.

The reality is, children are resilient and don't require as much as we think. They need clothes, a roof, and recreation but above all they need love. Mommying to life is really acknowledging that our children were entrusted to us but they belong to God. Just like we have a purpose, so do they. The best way we can serve our children is by making sure that we are healthy and well. I often do an assessment check of my mind, body, and soul. I rate them each by a percentage so I can see which part of me needs to be nurtured. If my mind seems low, I read or check in with my therapist. If my body is tired, I drink more water and be more conscious of my diet and activities. And if my soul feels weary, I plug into the ultimate source. I pray more and dig deep into the Word. Self care is truly the antidote for mommying to death. And God gives us permission to do so.

1 CORINTHIANS 6:12 NKJV

"All things are lawful for me, but all things are not helpful. All things are lawful for me, but I will not be brought under the power of any."

PRAYER

Heavenly Father,

You are the one true God. You are all things good and I thank You for blessing me with the honor and responsibility of being a mom. Help me to guide and train them up in the way that they should go. Merciful God, help me to remember that I cannot be all things to all people; even my children. That title only belongs to You.

In Jesus' name, amen.

CLEANSING THOUGHT

I'm not gonna go so far as to say "F them kids" but really, the kids are fine. And they're even better when their mother is happy and whole. As long as you drain yourself dry you won't have anything left for your children. The goal is to pour into yourself enough to overflow for the benefit of your children. Teach them how to value themselves by valuing yourself.

1. Without shame, list some difficulties of parenting?
2. How could our society do a better job supporting parents spiritually, mentally and physically?

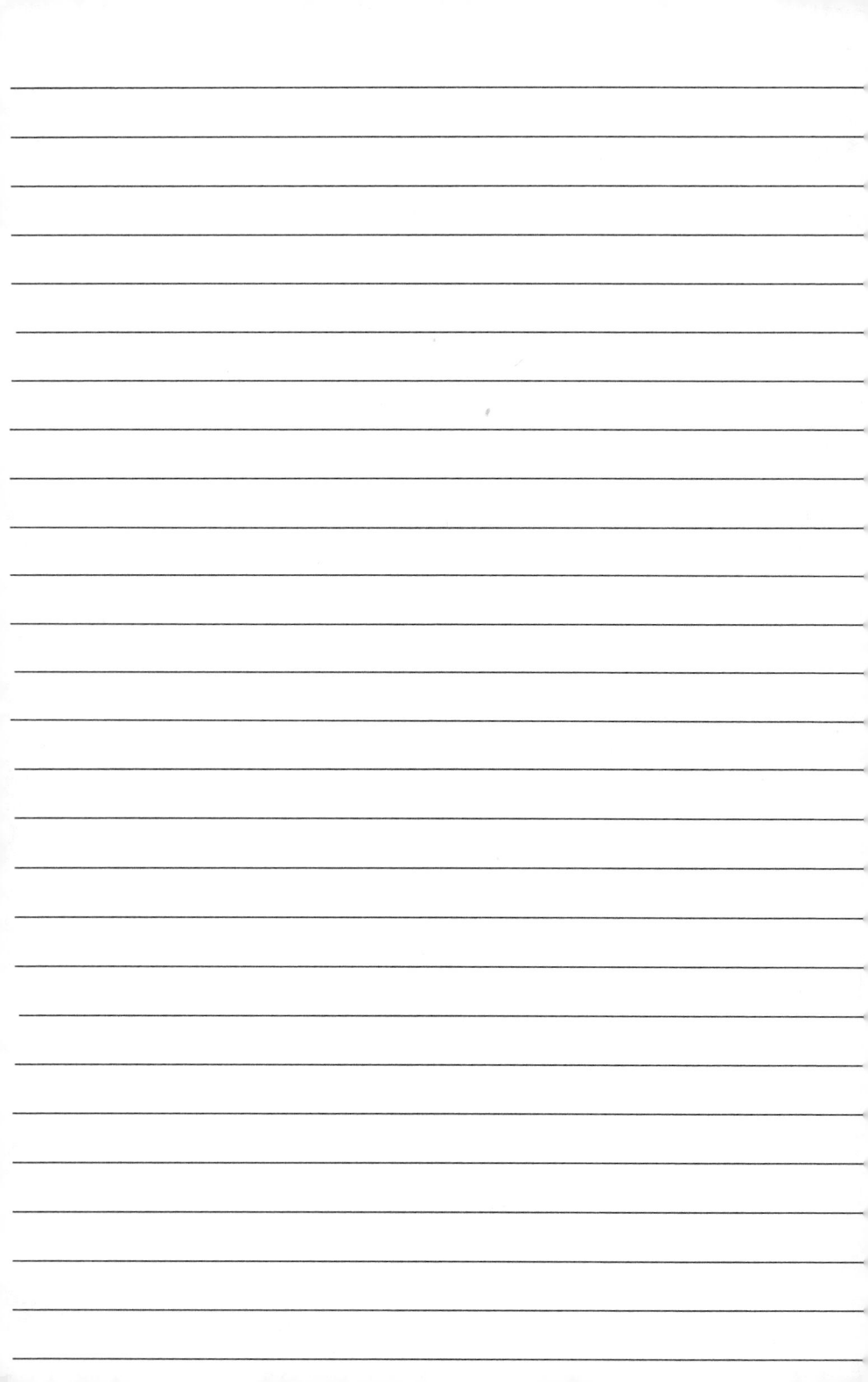

25

HAPPY - SAVED - HOT MESS - TRIGGER

I magine a nice, sunny morning. It's 78 degrees and the birds are chirping. Pure comfort floods the air as you open the door to take on the day. Your favorite morning drink is in your hand as you make way to your car. You're on time and wearing your favorite shoes. They feel so good on your feet as you walk with the power and authority God blessed you with. You get in the car, confident that you haven't forgotten anything today. You didn't have to rush. The gas tank in your car is full. How can a morning be so perfect? As you turn up the music, excited to hear the potential soundtrack to this beautiful morning, you hear a familiar song. And just like that your morning is ruined.

This song is connected to a not so perfect memory. Your ex played this song on repeat as he smelled like another woman's perfume. You no longer smell your fresh brewed Keurig but your car is now suffocating you with your ex husband's mistress' perfume. Now your stomach hurts and your hands get shaky. Whatever safety you felt has faded and now you feel insecure and broken. The air is congested and everything sucks. You've experienced a known assassin. You've been triggered.

Merriam-Webster defines trigger as, "to cause an intense and usually negative emotional reaction in (someone)." When I say the devil was slick as oil when he started using triggers to attack people. The most frustrating point of triggers is they don't always present themselves as negative because they hide in innocent pieces of our lives. They come in the form of songs, phrases, smells, foods, colors, places, and the most minuscule of things. Triggers have the power to undo a perfect day and truly disturb a perfect night of rest. They are tied to truly traumatic events and memories and sometimes ignite pain that appeared to be healed. The example I used of a trigger is just one of many. Some people are triggered concerning more serious situations like the death of a child, sexual abuse, undergoing chemotherapy, or even surviving a near death experience.

In 2020, where everything has been thrown at us including the kitchen sink, we were trigger happy. With the pandemic, social injustice and personal circumstances, there were almost no days off when it came to being triggered. What can we do to prevent this? Triggers are nothing more than fear. Outside of a respectable reverence, fear is not of God. God gave us many tools on how to handle fear in His word. I think because we have new terms for old problems, a lot of times we don't know how to combat them. We also have to reroute ourselves to live in the present. Triggers love to drag us backwards. If we have to say the affirmation, "I'm here, right now, in this space" to not be sucked into the downward spiral of a trigger then so be it. The devil is a liar and loves to use our past to disarm us. Declaration and prayer is the answer and that's the trigger we should pull.

PROVERBS 1:33 NIV

"But whoever listens to me will live in safety and be at ease, without fear of harm."

PRAYER

Father God,

My protector, please protect me from myself. Protect me from self-inflicted anxiety. I cannot change the past but I'm expecting You to give me the strength to accept it and grow from it. I rebuke negative thoughts and triggers that take me back to where you have brought me from. I invite a newfound strength and courage to navigate my life boldly and bravely, free from crippling memories.

In Jesus' name, amen.

CLEANSING THOUGHT

Our natural reaction to events that plague us is to be reactive. We walk around bracing ourselves for impact and being weighed down by anxiety. That's not the way a child of the King should move. The best reaction is to be proactive. We have authority given to us by God and doubled down by Christ to be courageous against the thief called fear. True freedom comes where fear ends and practice surely makes perfect.

1. Identify 3-4 things that trigger you.
2. Now look at each of the things you listed and identify the root of your trigger. Begin to work through the root issue in order to heal.

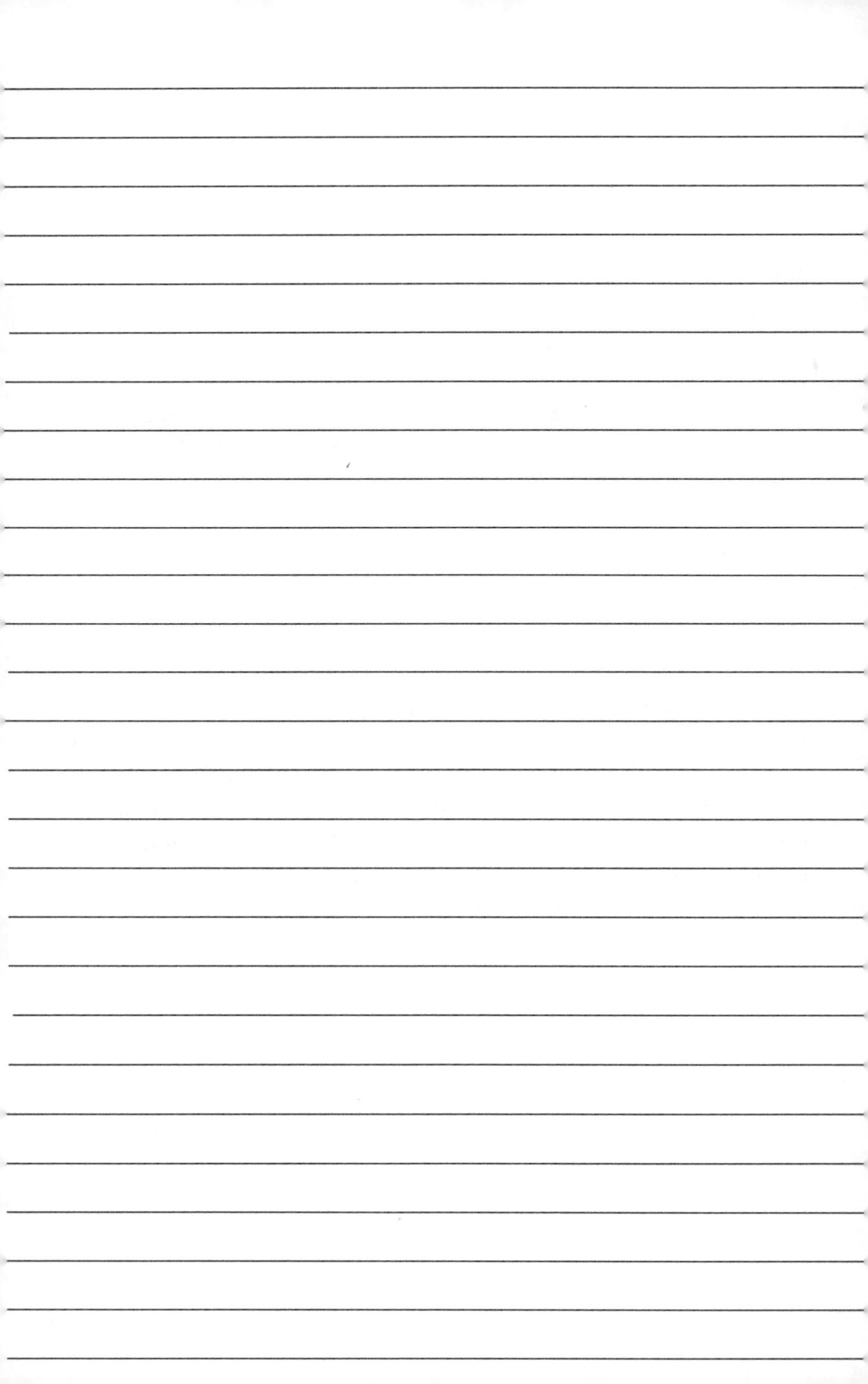

26

O nce before, I escaped the grips of death at the edge of hope. I carefully thought out the pros and cons of my life. I weighed my value alive vs. no longer alive. I convinced myself that this world would be better without me in it. So sparing the details, I tried to take my own life. I attempted suicide. Thank God I wasn't successful and am here to tell the story. My actions were a direct result of too much world and not enough God. The world measured me on conditions. Was I on my best behavior? Was I good enough in comparison to others? Did I have what it took to get through the things that were in front of me? Did anyone really care?

All of those questions would have never posed themselves if I had the wisdom to put my problems in God's hands. But I put them in the world's hands and felt what the world had to offer...quick, microwaved thrills that didn't have enough substance to hold me up in my time of need. I was on the edge of hope. Just a few walks towards hope would've pulled me out. The things that I could see at the time clouded my mind in such a tragic way I couldn't even fathom the beauty of what was unseen. If I could give any advice to anyone who isn't sure if living is worth it anymore, it's to just for a moment, hope again. I know those bills are tangible and building up faster than they can be paid but what if they could be paid by hope? I know the heartbreak that people claimed you would be over still feels fresh. You're spiritually bleeding all over the place but what if hope was the stitch to mend it? I know your mistakes feel amplified and are now what people see when they look at you, but what if hope could be your clean slate? I'm here to confirm for you that hope is the answer. It is real. Hope led me to faith and saved my life. The only catch is I had to be open to it for it to help me. So please, grab my hand and come off of that ledge. Experience hope in its full potential so if you're battling on the edge, it can save you, too.

JOB 3:3-4; 11-13 NLT

"Let the day of my birth be erased, and the night I was conceived. Let that day be turned to darkness...Why wasn't I born dead? Why didn't I die as I came from the womb? Why was I laid on my mother's lap? Why did she nurse me at her breasts? Had I died at birth, I would now be at peace. I would be asleep and at rest."

PRAYER

Dear God,

Please hear my cry! My thoughts are suffocating me. I can't breathe and I need you. Help me to regain hope and a reason for living. I'm having a hard time seeing myself the way You see me. I rebuke Satan and his grips over my life in Jesus' name. I invite Your light into every dark place in my heart, mind, and spirit. Lord grant me the strength to overcome this turmoil and be a living testimony to your grace.

In Jesus' name, amen.

CLEANSING THOUGHT

In 2020, an average of 132 Americans died by **suicide** each day. 1.4 million Americans attempted **suicide**. Anyone who is battling this demon should know they're not alone based on these statistics. It's so isolating; feeling like you want to die. My own experience used to be so hard to talk about. However, there was so much healing in opening up about it. Even with the story of Job, I knew he was an overcomer, but to know that he too no longer valued his life made me feel more human. It gave me hope to know that his story ended in prosperity and hope was the reason. [2]

If you or someone you know struggles with suicidal thoughts, you do not have to do it alone. Please reach out to the National Suicide Prevention Lifeline @ 800-273-8255.

---

1. The first step to stepping away from the edge of hope is gratitude. List at least 5 things you are grateful for.
2. Make a list of all of the things that make you feel hopeless. Put a line through the things you cannot change. Circle the things you can. Put a plan in action to change those things you circled.

---

[2] Suicide facts & Figures: United STATES 2020 - CHAPTERLAND.ORG. (n.d.). Retrieved from https://chapterland.org/wp-content/uploads/sites/13/2017/11/US_FactsFigures_Flyer.pdf

27

THE LAST TIME - SAVED HOT MESS - THIS IS

I usually tell myself this before I walk into a situation that I've already been in knowing I'll get the same result. And whether the result is even worth it, I still have to do it just once more. A lot of us can relate to being drunk as a skunk. The headache, the room spinning, vomiting, embarrassment, and the lack of awareness makes us say we will never drink again. Then the next holiday comes around...and tah dah! You're drinking again! I can personally relate to having a hard time letting go of something so sweet, so easily attainable, and is a delicacy to strong women.

I have a hard time letting go of...toxic men. As I finalize our bootleg plans through text, I'll tell myself, "This is my last time messing with him. It's like I know they're toxic and mean me no well, but there's something that draws me to them. There's an infatuation, curiosity and obsession with their spontaneity. I don't know if it's from the lack of responsibility but it feels like a free fall. And for a woman that lives with a lot of rules and order, that feels good. Like really good. Escape good. High good.

In all actuality, that free fall is a cheap, temporary feeling. It is meaningless and short lived. Sometimes, our urgency to get back to it is a testament to it's worth. Expensive taste and high value priced items and experiences take time and work and aren't easily accessible. Therefore you enjoy it and use the best judgment so you won't forget it. $3 shots and a man that will hound you about not answering his texts are plentiful. So why do we let cheap things take up space and energy in our destiny? And why are we lying to ourselves and God claiming this is the last time? What if there is no next time? Life is not promised. Happiness is not promised either. The only thing we are promised is death. It's a dark reality but it's the truth. We have to make our lives count. It's really hard to severe ties with anything we love. But if it no longer serves us, we must.

ROMANS 6:12-14 NKJV

"Therefore do not let sin reign in your mortal body, that you should obey it in its lusts. And do not present your members as instruments of unrighteousness to sin, but present yourselves to God as being alive from the dead, and your members as instruments of righteousness to God. For sin shall not have dominion over you, for you are not under law but under grace."

PRAYER

Gracious God,
I love you even when I don't obey. I know you don't bless me just for me to be hard-headed. Temptation and temporary fulfillment have become more important to me than serving You. Please help me to turn away from these bad habits. I want everything You have for me and won't let the distraction of sin get in my way.
n Jesus' name, amen.

CLEANSING THOUGHT

God is not blessing entanglements! (For the people in the back) Nor is He blessing us for us to keep bumping our heads in the same spot over and over again. Instead of taking my word for it, finish up Romans 6:12-23. Issa mic drop.

1. What is something that you left at the altar but went back to pick up a time or two?
2. Identify why the last time is never the last time and pray for deliverance from the root of the sin.

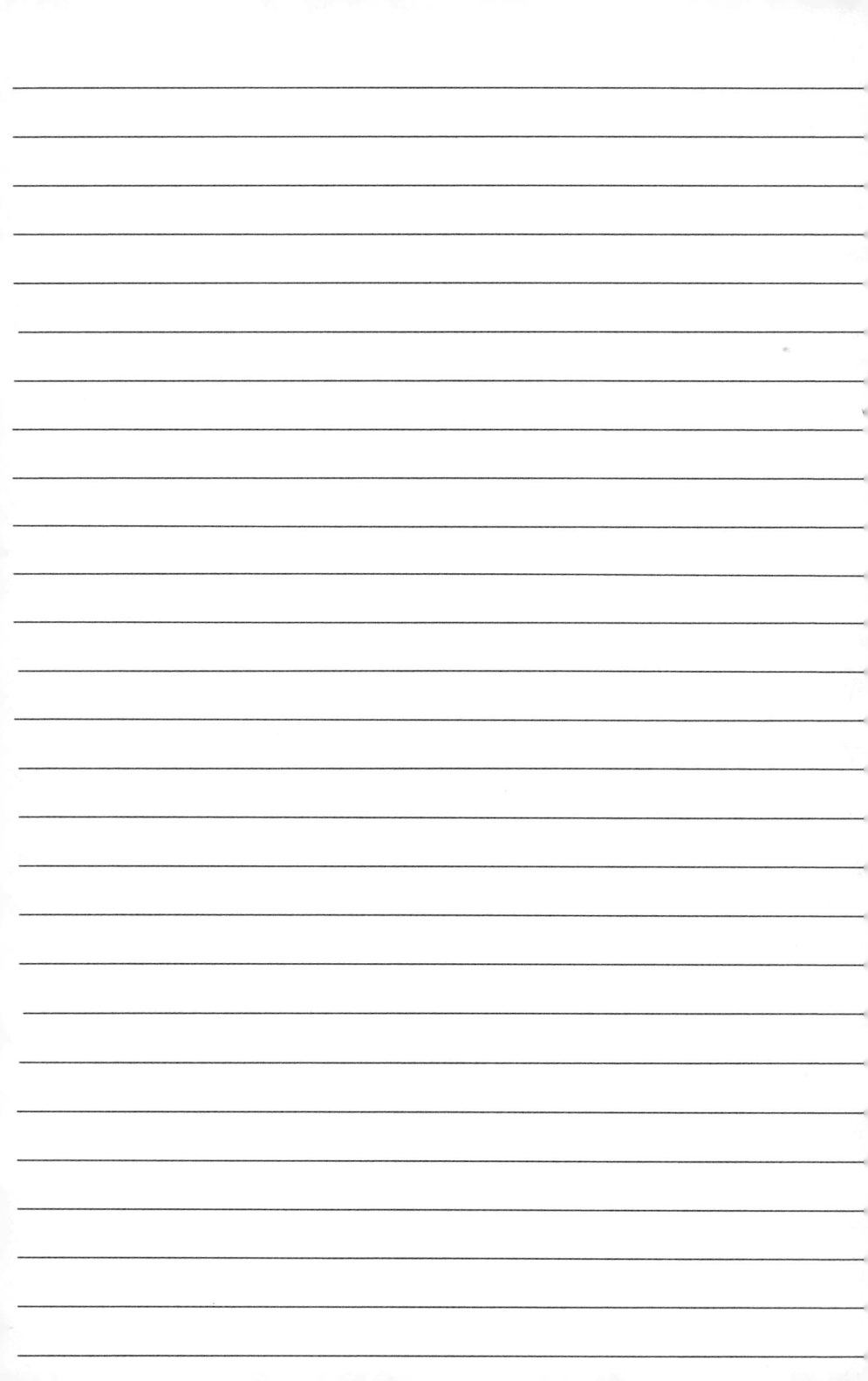

28

We made it to day 28 y'all! The most beautiful thing about this devotional is that it was written by a real life hot mess...me. I wrote the majority of this book from my iPhone. While maneuvering divorce court and adjusting to the new norm since the onset of my first pandemic, God gave me the bright idea to write a devotional. Many nights I deemed myself unqualified. I'm not a pastor or a minister. I'm not verified and barely a part of a church home. All I had was a tattered past, a heart of gold, and dreams. But hear me when I say, God knows how to use the most overlooked parts of us. Traits we consider insignificant are the very ones God uses the most. He wants you, all of you. See, in order for others to be drawn to Him, they sometimes have to see themselves. We are most connected by our human experiences. So in short, one hot mess can attract another (I got you to read this book right?)

All jokes aside, there's use for your pain and experiences in the kingdom of God and I'm here to affirm you in that. Proof of my theory is the way Jesus selected His disciples. He selected the basic, the sinful, and the wayward by society standards. They were pivotal pieces to the prophecy that saved us all. A hot mess is merely someone who doesn't measure up but shows up. There are so many hot messes in our history that have changed the trajectory of tragedy. They've stopped wars that plagued us and started wars to defend us. Hot messes have loved the unlovable and went against those with undeserved adoration. Hot messes have carried children at 16 that would become game changers of our society. Hot messes are history and aren't going anywhere anytime soon.

As the first member of the saved hot mess club, I am very much a hot mess and very much saved. It definitely feels confusing to not fit into the standard for Christians but have a heart for the work of Christ. God chose me regardless of how anyone might feel about it. And He chose you, too. There's work for us to do, beloved. Acknowledging our identity is not an excuse to be lukewarm and stagnant. There's kingdom work to be done. My challenge to you is to go up from here. Wherever you are starting, go upward and take someone with you. Keep going until you can say, "I used to be a hot mess so I can relate, but I'm set free in Jesus Christ."

Live long and love longer.

MATTHEW 9:11-13 NLT

"But when the Pharisees saw this, they asked his disciples, "Why does your teacher eat with such scum?" When Jesus heard this, he said, "Healthy people don't need a doctor-sick people do." Then he added, "Now go and learn the meaning of this Scripture: 'I want you to show mercy, not offer sacrifices.' For I have come to call not those who think they are righteous, but those who know they are sinners."

PRAYER

Eternal Father in Heaven,
Thank you for loving me in all my mess. You've loved me unconditionally regardless of my sins. Thank you for giving me beauty for ashes. I *am* a saved hot mess. I claim your salvation but live in sin. Please forgive me and help me to be a better steward of Your Grace. Help me be a better example to those who need You.

I love you so much.

In Jesus' name, amen.

CLEANSING THOUGHT

If I don't leave you with anything else, it is this:
I am not giving you permission to remain lukewarm. There is beauty in realizing and accepting who you are and where you are. However, it is not our destiny to stay there. As the kingdom of God expands, so shall our love for His purpose, obedience to His will, and the flock we attract to Him. He loves you and so do I.

1. Recall a time when you were a hot mess, saved or not.
2. Now repeat after me, "Even in my hot mess...Jesus loved me. He cared for me. His purpose was to save me!"

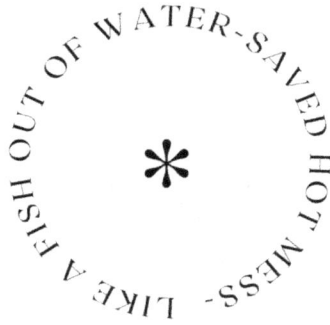

WATER-SAVED HOT MESS - LIKE A FISH OUT OF

*

True Story...

"You can't have a devotional for the imperfect without discussing church hurt."

aved Hot Mess was already finished when my publisher said this to me. As much as I wanted to be done with the writing process, I had to get back into the lab. Although I've had my own share of church hurt, I wanted to see what the Bible said about this sensitive topic.

My parents were Muslim, so the first 5 years of my life I was taught the principles of Islam. If I went to a sleepover with family or friends, they even sent my prayer rug. My first impression of religion was rooted in modesty, respect, and discipline. When my parents divorced, my mother decided to take a step back from organized religion and told my brother and me to find our own paths. So as I would spend the night with friends on the weekend, I would naturally go to church with them that Sunday.

My hometown is within the Bible Belt so most of my friends were Baptist. That's how I learned about Jesus. The experiences I had were so exhilarating from the powerful preaching and fellowship. The music would search my soul like no other.

I began my church hunt in my early twenties and finally found a church home of my own. And without the obligation from a big mama or tradition from a family, I became a part of a beautiful ministry. I attended church every Sunday, got baptized, joined the choir, attended Bible study, got married, got my children involved in children's ministry, and devoted my time and life into my church. The relationships I formed were more like family and that hit different for me. I have a history of a broken family. I never got to experience a doting grandmother on either side. My church had granny's-o-plenty! My church family even supported my business so it was only right that I began to tithe regularly. All my boxes were checked. I couldn't understand why my mother didn't want to join a church. Well, all that glitters isn't gold.

My church went through a very rough patch when my beloved pastor, the first I'd ever had, made a decision to move south with his family. With a history of abandonment issues, I was heartbroken. He was definitely the glue that held everything together. The silver lining was, I no longer had a crutch between God and me. I was forced to strengthen my relationship with God for myself. I matured spiritually through that process. As we got our new pastor, our entire church was hopeful indeed, but my home life began to fall apart. My husband and I started having severe marital problems and our finances were not stable. After rounds of counseling and praying we made the decision to divorce. The split was awful and I really needed my support system; my church, to cover my family as we navigated the muddy waters of divorce. I anticipated the women's ministry saving me and the men's ministry saving my husband. I waited for the pastor to come to my house and pray with me and my children. I waited for calls of support. I had a fairytale in my head of what healing would look like for me and it very much included my church. But that didn't happen.

Most of my church family was awkwardly silent. My mother's words to me were:

"And that's why I never took you to church," my mother said. "Bunch of hypocrites! When I divorced your father, the nation was very helpful and supportive to me and my children."

I felt bamboozled. For years I jumped out of my seat and clapped when I heard the preacher say, "We need to fellowship so we won't be alone. A person without a church is like a fish out of water."

So why did I feel like a fish out of water still? My name was added to a long list of people who considered themselves hurt by the church. Now, I still did have support and a handful were members but it wasn't the members I expected. It wasn't the overly righteous that came to my aid. It was the peculiar ones. The ones who got side eyed for short skirts or maybe were written off for not fitting in. They prayed for me, gave my children and me necessities, and regularly checked in on us. I also found great solace in my therapist. Even with the blessings God sent through the people that were present, I was still waiting for leadership at my church to come save the day. I saw my church adopt schools and other families throughout the years so I was curious as to why they didn't do the same for me. I started to throw a spiritual tantrum. My first bone to pick was with God.

"God! Why would you let all this happen to me? You gave me a husband just to let him slip away! You let me love people that would betray me. Why have you forsaken me?" I literally screamed.

I was low. I couldn't eat, was filled with disgust, and still felt obligated to be in church. I loved church so much. I felt like I was betraying myself by loving something so much that hurt me. As resentment settled into my spirit, the pandemic hit. So here was another mountain to climb and I wasn't even over the first one! Hope seemed frivolous at times.

My story is just one of many who felt betrayed by church. There are millions of people with stories so deep and demented it's hard to accept that believers could even be a part of it. Abuse, neglect, betrayal, jealousy, and many other sins are on this earth and sometimes can be concentrated right inside of the church. I was so oblivious and naive to it all. I was so broken the only person I could relate to was Jesus.

He had suffered, was wounded, and betrayed. As hurt as I was, my pain was not comparable to the pain He must've felt. And yet He still prayed for those who hurt Him and kept going to fulfill His purpose. No one on earth has experienced church hurt at the capacity that our Lord and Savior has. This is exactly why we should turn to Him when we feel hurt by people we love the most. There's beauty in betrayal. We wouldn't have had Jesus' resurrection had it not been for Judas' betrayal.

I dare you to find the beauty in your feelings of betrayal. Prayer, fasting, meditation, reading the word and opening up to faithful and loving believers helped me out of my rut. Once I found the beauty in my own betrayal, it brought me closer to God in the most intimate way and gave me the softest place to land.

MARK 15:33-34 NIV

"At noon, darkness came over the whole land until three in the afternoon. And at three in the afternoon Jesus cried out in a loud voice, "Eloi, Eloi, lema sabachthani?" (which means "My God, my God, why have you forsaken me?")

LUKE 23:34 NKJV

"Then Jesus said, "Father, forgive them, for they do not know what they do." And they divided His garments and cast lots."

PRAYER

Eternal Father,
Thank you for loving me endlessly. While I am grateful for Your love, I've been hurt by my church. I don't know why but this hurt hurts more than normal. I've allowed resentment, pain, and malice to overcome me. I'm giving it all to You. Allow forgiveness to overflow in my heart. Help me to understand the purpose of my pain. I want to use it to glorify You.
In Jesus' name, amen.

CLEANSING THOUGHT

Church hurt is a controversial topic. It can cause ongoing debates, rip apart friendships and families, and even turn followers away from Christ. Nothing is too much for God. He can still be glorified through church hurt. If you or anyone can relate to this topic, be gentle and patient. Allow the hurt person to have a voice but understand it is not a place to stay and dwell in. Hurt people are prone to hurt others. Let's make the devil mad by encouraging more unity where church hurt tried to divide.

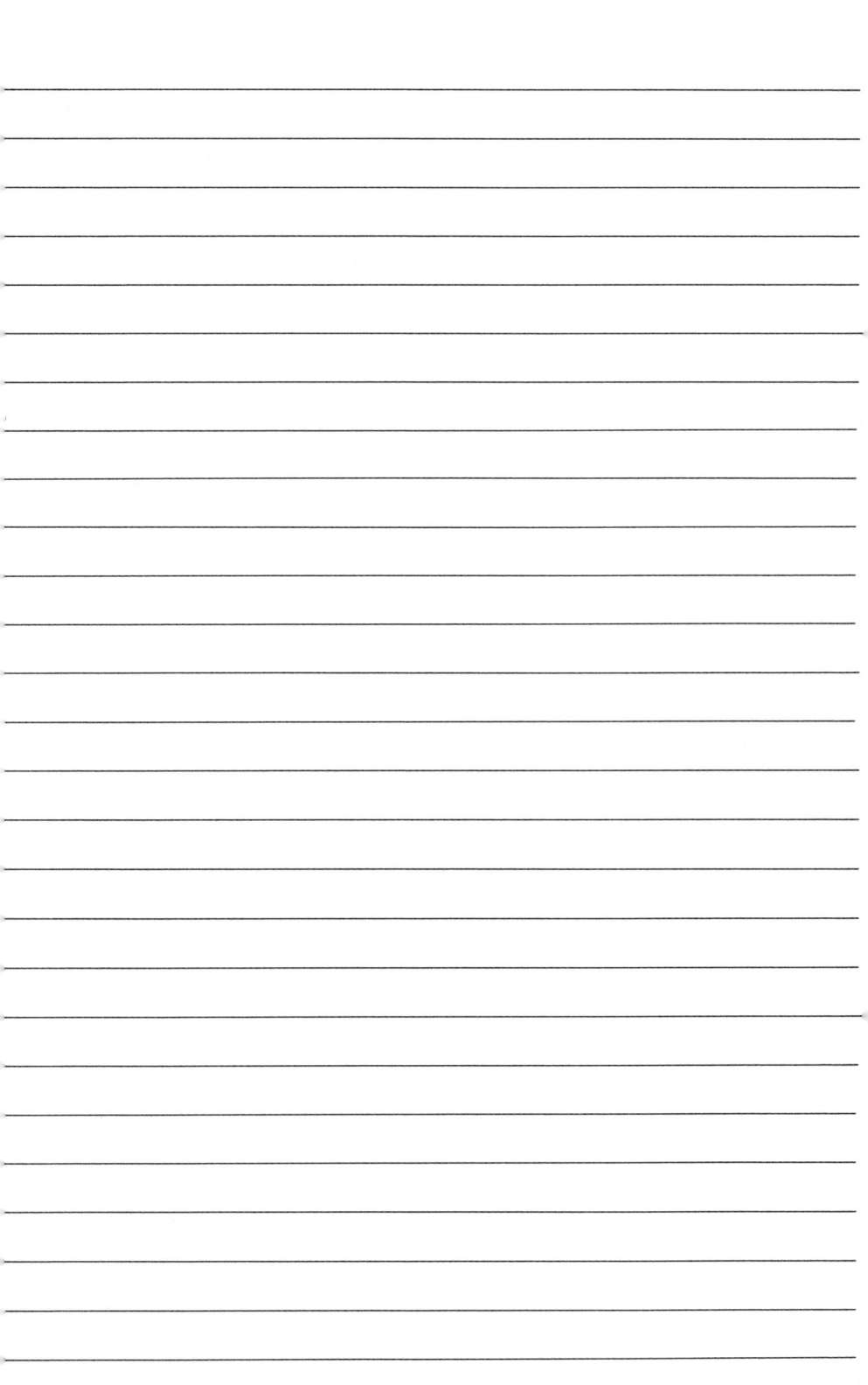

www.ingramcontent.com/pod-product-compliance
Lightning Source LLC
Chambersburg PA
CBHW071755090426
42737CB00012B/1830